The
Slow Cooker
Baby Food
Cookbook

The Slow Cooker *Baby Food* Cookbook

125 Recipes for Low-Fuss, High-Nutrition, and All-Natural Purees, Cereals, and Finger Foods

Maggie Meade
author of
The Wholesome Baby Food Guide

HARVARD COMMON PRESS

Inspiring | Educating | Creating | Entertaining

Brimming with creative inspiration, how-to projects, and useful information to enrich your everyday life, Quarto Knows is a favorite destination for those pursuing their interests and passions. Visit our site and dig deeper with our books into your area of interest: Quarto Creates, Quarto Cooks, Quarto Homes, Quarto Lives, Quarto Drives, Quarto Explores, Quarto Gifts, or Quarto Kids.

First Published in 2018 by The Harvard Common Press, an imprint of The Quarto Group, 100 Cummings Center, Suite 265-D, Beverly, MA 01915, USA.
T (978) 282-9590 F (978) 283-2742 QuartoKnows.com

The Harvard Common Press titles are also available at discount for retail, wholesale, promotional, and bulk purchase. For details, contact the Special Sales Manager by email at specialsales@quarto.com or by mail at The Quarto Group, Attn: Special Sales Manager, 401 Second Avenue North, Suite 310, Minneapolis, MN 55401, USA.

23 22 21 20 19   1 2 3 4 5

ISBN: 978-1-55832-908-9

Digital edition published in 2019

Library of Congress Cataloging-in-Publication Data available

Design: Claire MacMaster, barefoot art graphic design
Photography: Glenn Scott Photography
Styling: Natasha Taylor
Printed in China

The information in this book is for educational purposes only. It is not intended to replace the advice of a physician or medical practitioner. Please see your health-care provider before beginning any new health program.

Dedication

This book is dedicated to all parents and caregivers who struggle with what to feed their kiddos and if they are doing it "right." Do not fear, your babies will grow up strong and healthy because of all of your feeding efforts. It doesn't matter if you can't cook like Gordon Ramsay, and it won't be horrible if, once in a blue moon, you resort to the fast food drive-thru. You are amazing and doing it right—believe it! And to Gramma Jay-Jay, I will forever miss, love, and be thankful for you.

Contents

Introduction

Slow-cooking our food has been around for centuries—and feeding babies, well, that's been happening even longer. In this book, we combine a fabulous and convenient way to cook (in most cases, simply add a few fresh, whole ingredients to a slow cooker, set the heat level, and walk away!) with new and wonderful ways to feed babies as they transition from a diet of breast milk and/or formula to the amazing, tasty world of solid foods.

Transitioning babies to a diet of solid foods is never completely simple and smooth, not even for pediatric professionals. It can be a stressful time for parents, especially when you throw in the current 24-7 availability of parenting advice—much of which offers conflicting views. Plus, we're more time crunched than ever, so who has time to prepare a separate meal for baby? Yet many parents have concerns about serving their babies packaged, processed foods. And with good reason: homemade baby food retains more nutrients than packaged baby foods designed for a long shelf life. Plus, by making your own baby food, you're able to control the quality of the ingredients and their freshness. But that's not all. Check out chapter 1 for additional benefits of homemade baby food.

This book offers parents a sane and simple method of cooking for baby *and* the entire family, at the same time. More than just a book of baby food purees, this guide offers a broad range of recipes suitable for babies of all ages and stages, easily made in one appliance. Cooking foods for everyone in the family, in the same pot, eases the pressure placed on busy parents to feed their kids healthy, wholesome, and nutritious meals that don't come from a package, a pouch, or a jar. With recipes suitable for babies just starting out on solid foods, this book makes a progression from first foods to finger foods and on to meals suitable for older babies, toddlers, and the entire family.

With this book, parents don't have to spend hours each day preparing homemade baby foods, and they don't have to rely on jars or plastic pouches filled with industrially processed pureed foods to feed their babies. Making baby food in a slow cooker is a brilliant and convenient method of cooking for babies while cooking for the whole family. The slow cooker allows parents to prep the food, fill the cooker, and go about their day while tasty, nutritious foods and meals cook. At the end of the day, a delicious and nutritious meal is ready to be served and portions are ready to be pureed for baby. It's a true win-win for busy parents *and* hungry babies!

PART ONE
Why Make Homemade Baby Food? And Why Use a Slow Cooker

1

Fundamentals of Preparing Homemade Baby Food

It's true that having a baby changes *everything*. From the moment you lay eyes on your little one, your world changes—for the better. You want to do everything you can to give your child the best start in life. You pace the floor at night getting your baby to sleep, babyproof your home, and spend endless hours breast- or bottle-feeding. So when your baby is finally ready to begin eating solid foods, you want to give him or her the best nutrition possible. While the thought of making your own homemade baby food might seem attractive, you're probably wondering how you could possibly find the time—and energy. After all, you live in the real world. You've got a home, a job, other family responsibilities. And finding time to sleep would be nice, too.

Why Homemade Baby Food?

Sure, popping open a jar of commercially made baby food is easy, and there are seemingly endless varieties, including "all-natural" and organic baby foods. So why would you want to take the time out of an already hectic day to make homemade baby food? The simplest answer is this: you're already cooking breakfast, lunch, or dinner for the rest of the family, and it's likely that some of those foods are "baby foods," too! Yes, why not cook for your baby, too? There's no need to prepare separate meals for baby, using separate utensils and cooking ware. Your baby is able to eat the same foods you make—from the same appliances and pots, pans, and baking sheets. No matter what you're preparing for your family, the odds are good that any of those foods can be reduced to a puree that's safe and tasty for baby to eat!

Of course, there may be some occasions when you would want to prepare separate foods for baby. Even so, you can do this in conjunction with prepping family meals or by stuffing the slow cooker before you head off to work or are away from home for the day. Cooking up batches of homemade foods for your baby in the slow cooker will allow you to keep a stash on hand so that you aren't constantly cooking foods for baby to eat.

The recipes in this book are especially wonderful because they offer tasty sauces, cereals, and meal solutions for the whole family to enjoy in one way or another. Whipping up some slow cooker mixed berries? Spoon some of the sauce over vanilla yogurt or vanilla ice cream. Who knew making homemade baby food could be so easy and delicious? Now you do!

There are a few important reasons why homemade is better:

Taste: Homemade baby food tastes like real food. Jarred baby food and baby food in pouches just can't compare to the taste of freshly cooked homemade foods. Ask yourself, would you rather eat a banana that has been freshly mashed in your bowl or eat a jar of bananas that has been industrially processed and sitting on a shelf for months?

Texture: Commercially processed baby foods have the smoothest and silkiest texture. This texture is difficult to replicate when you make homemade foods for baby, but that isn't a bad thing. Homemade baby food helps your baby adjust to the texture of real foods and takes away one more hurdle to jump through when you wean your baby to solid foods.

Nutrition: Homemade baby foods may retain more nutrients than commercial jarred or pouched baby foods. In a 2016 public health study from the University of Aberdeen, Scotland, researchers found that homemade infant foods prepared from recipes in the top baby-food cookbooks may contain up to 77 percent more nutrients than commercial infant foods. The study also found that making homemade baby food from scratch is typically less expensive than buying store-bought baby food. It is also noteworthy that homemade baby foods tend to contain a wider variety of fruits and vegetables than commercial baby foods.

Further, it has long been thought that fresh and frozen foods retain more nutrients than canned foods do because of the way these foods are processed. Cooking and draining foods causes the most nutrient loss, while freezing incurs the least amount of loss. Some foods that you make homemade might contain more nutrients than their jarred or pouched counterparts solely due to how the ingredients are processed.

Quality control: You are the quality-assurance manager. You know exactly where the food you are preparing and feeding to your baby has come from. Also, there is great peace of mind in knowing how and where the food that you feed your baby was prepared.

Variety: While commercial baby food has come a long way, the varieties of foods and combinations on the shelf are still limited. You won't find bananas mixed with avocado and applesauce on the shelf, nor will you find chicken and sweet potatoes mixed with apples and cinnamon on the shelves, either. This variety will help your baby develop an adventurous palate that will provide a lifelong joy of food exploration.

All or nothing: Finally, it's important to mention that if you decide to make homemade baby food, doing so is not an all-or-nothing choice. Many parents feed their babies a mix of both homemade baby foods and commercial foods. This mix-and-match approach gives baby the same tastes that the family eats while offering busy parents the convenience of popping open a jar or cutting open a pouch when needed. However, as you get more comfortable creating homemade foods for your baby, you'll start to look at the meals you're making for your family and think, "Is there anything here that I can feed to baby tonight?" You'll be surprised at the options.

Incorporating Baby Food Making into Your Routine

Fortunately, it's not hard to incorporate making baby food into your routine. Below are a few things to keep in mind before you get started.

Same-Day Baby Food Prep vs. Make-Ahead Baby Food Prep

As many parents start cooking for their babies, they begin to develop their own strategies and routines. One of the questions most often asked by parents is "Should I cook every day or cook a big batch of food and then store it?" The answer? Whatever works best for you. In fact, preparing baby's food can vary from one day to the next. Many moms and dads who work outside of the home find cooking and preparing large batches of foods (often on the weekends) to be the most convenient way to prepare baby food. Parents who stay at home with their babies may find that same-day baby food prep is easier for them. Same-day or make-ahead baby food prep is not a one-or-the-other type of commitment. One week you may have time to prepare large batches of foods, and the next week you may just grab a banana and mash it as you go.

Using a slow cooker will work beautifully with either of these methods of baby food preparation. If you are making a big pot of chicken stew, for example, you can feed baby some at mealtime and then set aside several portions to store in the refrigerator or to freeze for feeding later on.

What Tools Do You Need to Make and Store Homemade Baby Food?

Most new parents are shocked when I tell them they already have everything they need to make homemade baby food. This is often a game-changer. Here's what you'll need—I'm willing to bet you already have most, if not all, of these tools and appliances.

- ☐ Slow cooker
- ☐ Oven
- ☐ Stovetop
- ☐ Microwave
- ☐ Freezer
- ☐ Blender
- ☐ Hand mixer (optional)
- ☐ Immersion blender (optional)
- ☐ Food processor
- ☐ Whisk
- ☐ Potato masher
- ☐ Coffee grinder
- ☐ Pots and pans
- ☐ Cooking spoons and other cooking utensils
- ☐ Paring, carving, and slicing knives
- ☐ Ice cube trays
- ☐ Storage containers
- ☐ Freezer-safe storage containers
- ☐ Freezer-safe resealable plastic bags

Puree and Prep Homemade Foods for Babies

Once you've cooked the food that you're going to make into baby food, the next step is to create a puree, which is simply food that has been turned into a thin, smooth texture. It is created by blending or processing a food, typically a fruit or vegetable (or a meat), until it becomes thin and smooth. This is usually accomplished in a food processor or blender, or even with a hand mixer or immersion (stick) blender. Babies who begin to wean from breast milk or formula often begin the transition with pureed food. Pureed foods can be ideal first foods for babies because the texture of the foods makes them easy to digest and easy to spoon-feed, plus they offer baby a familiar texture.

Keep in mind, though, that babies don't always have to start with purees. In fact, baby's first foods can also be soft, mashed foods. In chapter 4, we'll discuss the spoon-feeding method versus the baby-led feeding method and the pros and cons of both.

Slow Cooker Basics

Your slow cooker will be your new best friend as you embark on making homemade baby food. So let's make some formal introductions. We'll start by looking at its many iterations throughout the centuries. It's fascinating to see how cooking methods have, in principle, remained the same and yet have been transformed by the development of appliance technologies. Instead of digging a pit and filling it with wet leaves or using a wet clay pot in a simple oven, we just plug in a slow cooker and use little labor and far less fuss.

What Is a Slow Cooker and How Does It Cook?

Various versions of the slow cooker appear in historical records throughout many cultures that date back many centuries. Asian, Middle Eastern, and Roman cultures used clay pots, as did the Spanish and French, to cook many of their meals. You could say that the clay pot was one of the first slow cookers that was an actual appliance. These clay pots were used to slowly cook meats, stews, vegetables, and broths. The pot was either glazed or unglazed, and most often, it was created from terra-cotta. Before it was placed into an oven, the clay pot would be soaked in water for about 15 to 20 minutes. The foods would be added once the pot finished soaking. After the soaking and the addition of foods, the pot would then go into an oven to cook. Because clay is porous, the foods would slow-cook in warm moisture or steam and retain all their important nutrients and delicious, rich flavors.

Another ancient method of "slow cooking" that was used throughout the New and the Old Worlds was the open pit or earthen pit. Most cultures prepared their cooking pits using distinct methods, but all included digging a hole in the ground. After the hole was dug, hot rocks were added, followed by a layer of wet leaves or other plants such as seaweed. Native Americans in the Massachusetts Bay Colony area would dig a pit on the beach and fill it with hot rocks, a layer of seaweed, a layer of food, and finally another layer of seaweed. Dampened and moist plants created the warm steam that helped slow-cook the food and seal in flavor and nutrients.

Today's modern slow cookers bear little resemblance to those in the past. It is wonderful that we no longer have to go outside and dig a pit to cook our meals—unless we want to. The invention of the slow cooker has enabled busy families to enjoy delicious home-cooked meals that they may otherwise not have time to prepare and cook. The slow cooker is truly an appliance that every home should have.

Why Use a Slow Cooker?

Slow cookers provide a convenient and simple way to cook wholesome meals for the family, no matter what size family you may have. We're all busy, and finding the time to prep and cook a meal during the weekdays can be difficult. The slow cooker can save family mealtime from becoming a rotation of prepackaged foods and meals. Instead of having to rush home from work to spend valuable time prepping ingredients, using a slow cooker allows you to prep many ingredients for a meal the night before you cook. This pre-prep, alone, is a timesaver. In the morning, you add the ingredients to the slow cooker, turn it on, and then go about your day. Another great reason to use a slow cooker is that foods will stay tasty and nutritious. When cooked for the proper length of time, slow-cooked foods are tender, moist, and delicious. Plus, who doesn't love one-pot easy cleanup?

How Does a Slow Cooker Cook?

Slow cookers cook foods by evenly heating the food from the base up and along the sidewalls of the inner pot. Foods cook slowly and retain their moisture, and while steam is released from the slow cooker, it is the warm moisture that also helps to cook the food. This slow-cooking method helps retain nutrients, as well.

Types and Sizes of Slow Cookers

Slow cookers come in many shapes and sizes and have diverse types of controls. The following list of popular sizes will help you decide which size slow cooker may be best for your family and cooking purpose. Please note that for each quart, the slow cooker will hold four cups (945 ml) of water or other liquid.

- 1.5 quarts (1.4 liters): Best for dips or small portions of soups and stews.

- 2 quarts (1.9 liters): Good for two pounds (905 g) of chicken breast or other meats that are small in size. Also good for small portions of soups, stews, chili, vegetables, and fruit sauces.

- 4 quarts (3.8 liters): Great for three to four pounds (1.35 to 1.8 kg) of chicken or roast, soups, stews, chili, vegetables, fruit sauces, and desserts.

- 6 quarts (5.7 liters): Best for six pounds (2.7 kg) of chicken or roast, soups, stews, chili, vegetables, fruit sauces, and desserts.

Slow cookers also come in two basic shapes, round and oval, and the depth of a slow cooker may be shallow or deep. The oval shape is best for cooking large portions of meats such as a whole chicken or ribs. This shape is also great for cooking large portions of vegetables and for simmering fruit sauces. The round shape is often deeper than the oval, and it is best used for soups and stews and also may be used for cereals and fruit sauces. Many households have both round and oval slow cookers and use them for different types of recipes and meals. The same is true for the size of the slow cooker; many families own 2-quart (1.9 liter) as well as 4- or 6-quart (3.8- or 5.7-liter) slow cookers. The ideal slow cooker is the one that works best for each individual family's needs and meal styles. The best recommendation I can give you is this: buy a 2-quart (1.9 liter) and a 6-quart (5.7 liter) slow cooker and you will have all you need for any recipe you wish to prepare.

Types of Cooking Controls on Slow Cookers

There are two basic types of controls on slow cookers: electronic and manual. The electronically controlled slow cookers have more settings than the manually controlled ones. Here's what to know about each.

- Programmable: Low, high, and warm settings, as well as timer settings. When cooking is finished, switches to warm. Some models are also Wi-Fi enabled.

- Manual: Low, high, and warm settings. Must be manually controlled, does not automatically switch to warm, and no ability to set cooking time.

Best Methods of Cooking Foods in a Slow Cooker

Fruits: Cooking fruits in a slow cooker to make sauces or other types of fruity dishes is relatively simple. Most fruits should be peeled and seeded prior to placing them in the slow cooker.

Vegetables: Vegetables that are cooked in a slow cooker come out with a rich flavor as if they had been roasted in an oven. Generally, you should peel and seed the vegetable; however, there are a few vegetables that you can toss into the slow cooker whole. (For example, you'll find a recipe for whole butternut squash on page 60.)

Meats (raw or seared or braised): In the past, many chefs advocated that meats never be placed into a slow cooker raw and believed that meats should be seared or precooked first, mostly for food safety reasons. Personally, I seldom sear or precook meats when using a slow cooker; the few exceptions are when the recipe itself calls for it and I see the value of spending the extra time. Meats are brought above the recommended 160°F (70°C) temperature when they are slow-cooked for hours, and no food safety issue should be present.

Grains and pasta: Grains and pasta may be cooked in a slow cooker either alone or in a combination recipe. (Try the recipe for Overnight Buckwheat Cereal with Cinnamon Pears on page 144.)

Combination meals: Slow-cooking combination meals yields flavorful and nutritious meals for any size family. For the majority of recipes, all of the ingredients are added at once. Recipes that call for cheese or pasta may require the addition of these particular ingredients at a later time in the cooking process. The late addition of some ingredients helps to ensure that those ingredients aren't reduced to a soggy or unappetizing mess.

Slow Cooker Strategies for Feeding Baby and the Family

Preparing meals in a slow cooker is a convenient and delicious way to feed your family healthy, home-cooked meals with little fuss and time. It's also a simple and easy way to make homemade foods for your baby. One of the greatest things about making your baby homemade food is that you teach your baby about the tastes and textures of foods the family eats. Using a slow cooker to make foods and meals for the family that you can also use to feed your baby is a delicious and nutritious tactic.

When your baby is just beginning solid foods, you'll want to cook only single-ingredient foods and leave out herbs and spices for the first three or four weeks. But don't let the need for cooking single-ingredient foods stop you from using the slow cooker and creating a dish for the family, too. Many simple recipes for babies just starting to eat solid foods can easily be made into a side dish or a soup or an addition to a soup, stew, or casserole for the rest of the family. For example, the recipe for pumpkin on page 71 is one of these recipes; turn it into soup or pumpkin butter.

After the first three or four weeks, you should have a good idea of what foods your baby is tolerating and what foods may be causing digestive upsets or allergic reactions. With each new food you introduce, the opportunity to create more combination recipes with more ingredients increases. As you embark on this culinary adventure, remember that the tastes and textures you introduce early on will shape your baby's palate for the future.

3

Choosing Your Ingredients— And Serving Them Safely

One of the great advantages of making your own homemade baby food is that you get to choose exactly what goes into it—which means you control the quality. In this chapter, I'll give you tips on choosing the best ingredients your family can afford, plus advice on how to store, freeze, thaw, and reheat your finished food.

Organic vs. Conventional: Be Aware of the Differences

Organic foods or conventional foods? It's a question that causes a lot of anxiety for parents, especially when it's time to start their babies on solid food. Which type of food is more nutritious, and which is safer to feed to babies? To understand the differences, let's take a look at the two types of food growing practices:

Organic food. This is food that has been grown without the use of chemical pesticides, synthetic fertilizers, sewage sludge, or GMO/bioengineered seeds.

Organic meats, dairy, and eggs must come from animals that have not been given antibiotics or growth hormones. The feed the animals eat cannot contain animal by-products and must be vegetarian. It must not have GMO grains and cannot have been grown with conventional pesticides. The feed must also be free from antibiotics.

Conventional food. Conventionally grown food is or may be grown with chemical pesticides and fertilizers and also may be GMO or bioengineered. Conventional meats are from animals that may have been given growth hormones and/or antibiotics. The animals may also be fed food that contains animal by-products, and the food may be grown from GMO or bio-engineered grains and seeds. The grain-based feed can also have been treated with pesticides and/or fertilizers.

If you do choose to go the organic route, there are a few different organic labels to watch for. The USDA uses these standards to label organic foods:

"100 percent organic." This phrase can be used to label any product that contains 100 percent organic ingredients (excluding salt and water, which are considered natural). Most raw, unprocessed farm products can be designated "100 percent organic." Likewise, many value-added farm products that have no added ingredients—such as grain flours, rolled oats, etc.—can also be labeled "100 percent organic."

"Organic." "Organic" can be used to label any product that contains a minimum of 95 percent organic ingredients (excluding salt and water). Up to 5 percent of the ingredients may be nonorganic agricultural products that are not commercially available as organic and/or nonagricultural products that are on the National List.

"Made with organic _____." This phrase can be used to label a product that contains at least 70 percent organically produced ingredients (excluding salt and water). There are a number of detailed constraints regarding the ingredients that make up the nonorganic portion.

Specific ingredient listings. For products containing less than 70 percent organic ingredients, the specific organic ingredients may be explained in the ingredient list—for example, "Ingredients: water, barley, beans, *organic tomatoes*, salt."

Should Only Organic Ingredients Be Used to Make Baby Food?

The decision of whether or not to use organic foods to make baby food is an entirely personal one. Many parents will purchase only organic foods to feed their babies as well as their whole family. The benefit in making baby food with organic foods is that baby's exposure to conventional chemical pesticides and fertilizers is almost eliminated. During their first 12 months of life, babies consume a higher amount of fruits and vegetables relative to their weight, and in theory, this means they would be consuming more of the pesticides and chemicals found in conventional foods. It is a good idea to try to offer your baby as many organic foods as possible during their first 12 months to reduce the exposure to synthetic pesticides and fertilizers.

If you can't afford to feed your whole family a 100 percent organic diet, it's still beneficial to purchase and cook some organic foods. There are parents who use organic foods solely for baby's first food ingredients. On the other hand, many parents who make their own baby food will never buy any organic foods. While purchasing and cooking organic foods has many benefits, just cooking homemade foods for your baby gives your baby many advantages. If you are unable to find organic produce or simply cannot afford the higher price of organic food, you should still use fresh fruits and vegetables when making your own baby food.

"Keep Them on Hand" Ingredients

One of the secrets to being able to cook fresh homemade meals easily is to have a stockpile of ingredients always on hand. These ingredients range from herbs and spices to meats, frozen vegetables, and fresh fruits. Take this cook's secret and use it to help you cook up homemade baby foods along with tasty meals for the entire family. Here are a few ingredients you should try to keep in your cupboards, fridge, and freezer:

- Fresh fruits: apples, bananas, pears, peaches
- Fresh vegetables: carrots, green beans, peas, potatoes, winter squash (butternut, acorn)
- Frozen vegetables: mixed vegetables, green beans, winter squash (butternut, acorn), carrots, peas
- Frozen fruits: peaches, blueberries, mangoes, melon, and strawberries
- Canned vegetables: carrots, green beans, peas, tomatoes
- Meat (fresh and frozen)
- Fish
- Pasta
- Rice
- Oatmeal
- Barley
- Butter
- Eggs
- Cheese
- Milk: dairy, almond
- Herbs and spices

Pick and Choose: Getting the Most Value for Your Organic Buck

If you like the idea of using organic ingredients but can't afford to feed your family a 100 percent organic diet, the Environmental Working Group (EWG) creates a yearly list of the twelve conventionally grown produce items with the highest levels of pesticides ("The Dirty Dozen"). On the flip side, they also create a list of "The Clean Fifteen," which are the fifteen produce items that they've found have the lowest levels of pesticides. You can save money and still limit your family's exposure to pesticides by spending more for organic versions of the Dirty Dozen and buying conventional versions of the Clean Fifteen. Here are their lists for 2017. You can also check their website, ewg.org, for yearly updates.

The EWG's Dirty Dozen of 2017

1. Strawberries
2. Spinach
3. Nectarines
4. Apples
5. Peaches
6. Pears
7. Cherries
8. Grapes
9. Celery
10. Tomatoes
11. Sweet bell peppers
12. Potatoes

The EWG's Clean Fifteen of 2017

1. Sweet corn*
2. Avocados
3. Pineapples
4. abbage
5. Onions
6. Sweet peas (frozen)
7. Papayas*
8. Asparagus
9. Mangoes
10. Eggplant
11. Honeydew melon
12. Kiwifruit
13. Cantaloupe
14. Cauliflower
15. Grapefruit

*Note: A small amount of the sweet corn and papayas sold in the United States is produced from genetically modified seeds. If you want to avoid genetically modified produce, purchase organic varieties of this produce.

Ideally, when making homemade baby food, it's best to use fresh ingredients. However, it is perfectly acceptable, safe, and healthy to make meals from frozen foods as well. There are even some food and nutrition experts who believe that frozen foods may actually retain more nutrients than fresh foods. Picked at their peak of ripeness and freshness, frozen vegetables and fruits are flash frozen to retain all of their nutrients and flavor. Many companies that produce frozen foods will flash freeze their harvest right in the field. Unlike freshly picked foods, these frozen foods don't sit around in a warehouse or travel miles and miles in a truck that may or may not have proper refrigeration. Note that if you use frozen ingredients to make meals that you want to use for homemade baby foods, you can refreeze the foods once they have been cooked and pureed.

While canned foods are certainly not completely lacking in nutrition, they do lack in the full range of flavors and textures that fresh or frozen foods offer. Canned foods are processed at high temperatures to ensure that they will be safe for consumption and to allow them to sit on shelves for years, but unfortunately, this processing also strips away the real texture and flavor of the food. Many are also high in sodium. Whenever possible, try to avoid using canned foods when making homemade baby food.

Safe Food Preparation

Food safety is always important when you're cooking, but it takes on an added significance when you're making food for your baby and children. The fragile, still-developing digestive systems of babies are particularly vulnerable to food-borne pathogens and illness. Refer to the following guidelines for safe food handling, preparation, and storage according to the type of food.

Fruits and vegetables: It's important that you wash your hands before handling fruits and vegetables. All fruits and vegetables should be thoroughly cleansed prior to being prepared and cooked. Food safety experts all agree that simply washing your fruits and veggies under cool, clean running water is enough to get rid of residues, dirt, and bacteria. If the food has a firm surface, such as potatoes or apples, you might also scrub the surface with a brush. For extra assurance, you could wash produce with a mixture of vinegar and water, using three parts water to one part vinegar, or you can purchase a fruit and vegetable "wash" from the grocery store.

Meats, poultry, and fish: Always wash your hands before and after handling raw meats, poultry, and fish. It is also important that you use a separate cutting board for meat prep and a different one to prepare other foods. Try to complete prepping nonmeat items before you move on to preparing meat because this will reduce the possibility of contamination. This strategy will also minimize the number of times you must go back and wash your hands. To ensure safety, meats should be cooked to a specific internal temperature in accordance with the type of meat. Please refer to the following table when cooking meat, poultry, eggs, and seafood.

Safe Cooking Guidelines for Meat, Poultry, Eggs, and Seafood*

Category	Food	Temperature	Rest Time
Ground meat and meat mixtures	Beef, pork, veal, lamb Turkey, chicken	160°F (70°C) 165°F (75°C)	None None
Fresh beef, veal, lamb	Steaks, roasts, chops	145°F (65°C)	3 minutes
Poultry	Chicken and turkey, whole Poultry breasts, roasts Poultry thighs, legs, wings Duck and goose Stuffing (cooked alone or in bird)	165°F (75°C) 165°F (75°C) 165°F (75°C) 165°F (75°C) 165°F (75°C)	None None None None None
Pork and ham	Fresh pork Fresh ham (raw) Precooked ham (to reheat)	145°F (65°C) 145°F (65°C) 140°F (60°C)	3 minutes 3 minutes None
Eggs and egg dishes	Eggs Egg dishes	Cook until yolk and white are firm. 160°F (70°C)	None None
Leftovers and casseroles	Leftovers Casseroles	165°F (75°C) 165°F (75°C)	None None
Seafood	Fin fish Shrimp, lobster, crabs Clams, oysters, mussels Scallops	145°F (65°C) or cook until flesh is opaque and separates easily with a fork. Cook until flesh is pearly and opaque. Cook until shells open during cooking. Cook until flesh is milky white or opaque and firm.	None None None None

*Courtesy foodsafety.gov

Storage and Heating Tips for Baby Food Puree and Meals

Once you've served your homemade baby food (or your meal for the entire family), there are a few more things to keep in mind when storing the leftovers.

When Is It Safe to Store the Baby Food Puree?

You'll want to avoid putting any hot foods directly into the refrigerator or freezer. Doing so could change the temperature of the surrounding foods and cause a fluctuation of temperature in the appliance itself. While this isn't necessarily a far-reaching food safety issue, maintaining stored foods at a constant temperature will help stop bacterial growth. This is particularly important for baby foods because of a baby's immature and fragile immune system, which makes them more susceptible to food poisoning and illness, and it keeps the food fresh for a longer period of time.

So when should you put the cooked foods into the fridge or freezer? A simple rule to remember is the "Two to Cool" rule. Freshly cooked foods should not be left to cool at room temperature for longer than 2 hours. If possible, place the foods into the fridge within 1 hour if they have cooled. Bacteria begin to grow best after foods have been left out for longer than 2 hours, and they grow even faster if the room itself is warm or the foods are left outside in the heat. Keep in mind that the foods don't have to be cooled to the point where they are literally cold; cool, not hot, is the best way to store foods in the refrigerator, no matter who will be eating the food.

Refrigerator Real Estate: It's All about Location

Did you know there are specific areas in the refrigerator where certain foods should and shouldn't go? Use the following tips to organize your fridge so that your foods will maintain the most nutrition and health benefits.

Refrigerator doors: Store condiments and accompaniments on the doors, including ketchup, mustard, jams, jellies, and salad dressings. The doors are the warmest areas of the refrigerator.

Top shelf: Foods that don't really pose a health risk should be stored on the top shelf. The top shelf is the warmest area of the refrigerator, along with the doors. Jams and jellies, salsa, and canned drinks such as juices and seltzer waters are items that are good to store on the top shelf.

Middle shelf: Use this for foods that should maintain their cool temperature and are a higher risk than "top shelf" foods. These foods include eggs, milk, cheese, and even deli meats.

Bottom shelf: Always store fresh meats, poultry, and fish on the bottom shelf. When these foods are on the bottom shelf, the risk of their juices leaking and dripping down to contaminate other foods is minimized. The bottom shelf is also the coldest area of the fridge.

Drawers: The drawers are for storing vegetables and fruits. Some refrigerators have a deli drawer as well where you can store deli meats and cheeses.

Where Should Purees and Meals Be Stored and for How Long?

It is entirely your choice as to how and where you store your cooked and prepared homemade baby foods. The method that you choose to use for food storage will depend on what you want to do with the foods and how you plan on feeding them to your baby. If you make a large batch of food, splitting up portions and storing some in the refrigerator and putting some into the freezer may be the best option. If you make small portions to last for just a few days, then the best thing to do is to keep the foods in the fridge.

Refrigerator Storage

Follow these simple rules to ensure baby food safety.

- Always store homemade baby food in a BPA-free container that is tightly sealed.

- Store the container in the middle section of the refrigerator. This section of the fridge is colder than the top shelf.

- Homemade baby food purees should be stored in the refrigerator for no longer than 3 days.

- Saliva can contaminate and breed bacteria. Never re-store any foods in containers that baby has been directly eaten from in any way. If you don't think that your little one will eat a full portion, take out the amount you need and serve that.

Freezer Storage

Follow these simple rules to ensure food stays properly frozen:

- Cool foods prior to freezing.

- Freeze in individual portions to help make preparing small meals easier (see "Freezing Homemade Baby Food" on page 28).

- Store purees in the back of the freezer to maintain a constant frozen state.

- Be aware that purees tend to form ice crystals due to the liquid rising and separating from the food. These crystals are not freezer burn.

- Do not thaw, warm, feed, and then refreeze baby foods.

- Frozen baby foods keep well for 3 to 6 months in the freezer.

If you're storing your baby's food in a plastic container, make sure it's BPA-free. These containers are made without the industrial chemical bisphenol A, or BPA, which some studies have shown can seep into food and possibly cause negative health effects. Plastic containers that have the recycle codes 2, 4, and 5 are considered BPA-free.

Freezing Homemade Baby Food

One of the best things about making large batches of homemade baby food in your slow cooker is that you can freeze the leftovers to pull out on hectic days. This means that a few minutes of prep time combined with a few hours of (hands-off) cooking time can result in a freezer stocked with healthy, homemade baby food that's ready when your baby is.

It's especially convenient to freeze your baby food in serving sizes corresponding to his stage (which we'll discuss in the next chapter).

Stage One: Freeze food in 1-ounce portions to reduce waste. A standard ice cube tray is perfect for this. You could also use any container that is freezer safe. Once frozen, transfer the food into freezer-safe bags and label the bags with the date and the name of the food. Store in the back of the freezer for 3 to 6 months.

Stage Two: Freeze food in 2- to 4-ounce containers, depending on your baby's appetite. You can also use large ice cube trays. Once frozen, transfer the food into freezer-safe bags and label the bags with the date and the name of the food. Store in the back of the freezer for 3 to 6 months.

Stage Three: Freeze leftovers in a large freezer-safe resealable plastic bag and label with the date and the name of the food. You may want to freeze different foods from the same meal in separate freezer bags or containers. For example, if you have leftover Italian Wedding Soup (page 195), freeze some of the meatballs separately to be used later as part of a meal or mixed in with other foods; I love combining the meatballs with mac-n-cheese. Store in the back of the freezer for 3 to 6 months.

Thawing, Heating, and Serving Homemade Food

When it comes time to thaw, heat, and serve baby's meals, use the same methods that you use for big people food. There are a few ways to thaw baby foods that you can take advantage of:

- Remove the foods from the freezer and place them in the refrigerator until thawed; this is the best and safest way to thaw any food, although it is also the slowest method.
- Place frozen baby food cubes or meals in a microwave-safe container and defrost in the microwave, stirring frequently to avoid hot pockets and burning.
- Float food cubes in a container that is placed in a pot or a bowl of hot water.

Food safety experts say that you should reheat foods rapidly and bring the foods to a temperature of at least 165°F (75°C). This applies to all types of foods and is most important when you are reheating foods for baby.

To warm baby food, you can use the microwave or the stovetop. If you will be using the microwave to warm baby foods, heat them on high power in 20-second intervals and stir after each interval to prevent hot spots. Heating foods on high power will help to ensure food safety, and doing it at intervals will allow you to better control the temperature and help ensure that baby will not be burned by overly hot foods. To warm foods on the stovetop, just add the food to a pot, skillet, or saucepan and heat to an appropriate temperature.

Important: Before you serve any foods to your baby, please be sure to check the temperature of the foods. Always stir the foods thoroughly to prevent hot spots from burning your baby.

Travel with Homemade Baby Food

Believe it or not, it is relatively easy to travel with homemade baby food. You don't have to rely on commercially prepared baby foods to feed to your baby when you travel. Whether you're taking your little one out for a day at the beach or taking him on a long journey, there are several strategies you can use to take premade homemade foods with you. First, and simplest, is to take advantage of three fresh foods that travel well and don't need to be prepared ahead of time: bananas, avocados, and yogurt. Pack these foods—plus a fork, spoon, knife, and bowl with a lid—in a small cooler, and you have a meal or two wherever you may be. Peel the banana and slice or break off a few pieces, mash them up, and then serve. You can open the avocado and scrape out some of the flesh and mash it for baby's meal or a snack. Or you can even try a few spoonfuls of the yogurt with some of the banana and/or avocado mashed into it for a healthy meal on the go.

Another option for feeding baby on the go is to transfer some thawed baby food cubes to a covered bowl and pack it in a cooler with an ice pack or two. If you're at a restaurant, you'll find that most places will be happy to warm up the food for you or bring you a bowl of warm water to float the container of cubes in. Don't forget that the restaurant may also have something on its menu that baby can eat. Baked sweet potatoes or steamed veggies are often served without seasoning; just ask your server. You can also ask your server about other healthy, nonseasoned options for your little one.

4

Feeding Your Baby Solid Foods at Every Stage

One of the biggest milestones for a baby is the transition from a completely milk-based diet to eating solid foods. As with other milestones, such as learning to walk and talk, there are different stages your baby will go through on this journey. A few of the things to consider before you start this transition are your baby's age, physical maturity, and of course, what your baby's pediatrician recommends. When you begin the transition, it's important to learn about the kind of foods you'll want to start feeding your baby. In the pages that follow, we'll discuss the various stages of introducing solid foods and why it's best to introduce certain foods at specific ages. We'll also talk about allergies and digestive issues. Let's begin with the most important thing first: how to know when your baby is ready for solid foods.

When to Begin Feeding Solid Foods: Know the Signs

The American Academy of Pediatrics and health organizations worldwide recommend that babies begin to slowly move from milk-based feedings to solid foods around the age of 6 months. However, some pediatricians will give the okay to start babies on solids around 4 months of age. This is an important discussion to have with your baby's pediatrician.

In most cases, waiting until your baby is 6 months old to introduce him to the wonderful world of solid foods has many advantages and gives your child time to become physically ready to safely handle solid foods. Here are a few signs to let you know that your baby may be ready to begin solid foods:

- Good head control
- Has outgrown the tongue-thrust reflex (when a baby automatically pokes out his tongue when any unusual substance is placed on it, which keeps the baby from choking)
- Sitting up in a seat with very little assistance
- Frequent need for feedings
- Interest in the food on your plate
- Hand–eye coordination
- Strong pincer grasp (able to pick up bits and pieces with the thumb and finger)

These signs aren't meant to be absolute, and many babies display just two or three of them when they begin to eat solids. Of the signs mentioned, the three most important are good head control, the loss of the tongue thrust-reflex, and being able to sit in a seat with little propping or assistance. If your baby can't control her head, spoon-feeding her solids could be dangerous. If you must prop or recline your baby to feed her, there is a real possibility of choking or aspirating food.

Most importantly, if your baby still has an active tongue-thrust reflex, anything with texture and anything that is not a real liquid will be pushed right back out. The tongue-thrust reflex is an amazing survival adaptation. Without it, infants who are not old enough to make chewing motions and properly move textured substances around their mouths and away from the back of the throat could choke to death.

Food Before One, Just for Fun

As you start the transition to solid foods, remember the phrase "food before one is just for fun!" This doesn't mean that babies don't need to eat solid foods at all until they celebrate their first birthday. In fact, babies should start trying some solid foods around the age of 6 months because these foods will offer them additional nutrients, including vitamin C and iron, they need as they grow. The solid food transition is "fun before one" but also plays a crucial part in forming healthy eating habits as well as developing hand–eye coordination, learning how to self-regulate, and knowing how "full" feels.

What "food before one is just for fun" means is that you shouldn't stress that your baby isn't eating enough carrots or that she won't eat all of her beef puree at one meal. Your baby's main nutrition will still come from formula and/or breast milk, and the solid foods will supplement and complement that. There is no need to stress about the actual amounts baby is eating or worry that you should force baby to eat one more bite. Providing a well-rounded diet of fruits and vegetables and proteins will ensure optimal health and growth.

As baby gets older, solid feedings will increase, and baby will gain more and more nutrition from those solid foods. This is a natural progression. Before you know it, your healthy baby will be weaned off of milk feeds (likely as he enters into toddlerhood, though some continue to breast-feed longer) and eating meals right along with the family!

Speaking of survival adaptations, did you know that humans are born to dislike the taste of bitter foods and liquids? This innate dislike of bitter flavors is meant to protect us from eating poisonous plants and substances. You won't find too many poisonous plants with lovely sweet tastes.

Food Allergies, Intolerances, and Reactions

Once you determine that it is time to begin introducing baby to solid foods, it's important that you gain an understanding of food allergies and how they can impact this transition. The good news is that most babies outgrow food allergies by the time they are 3 or 4 years of age.

Food allergies can occur anytime and with any food. Even foods that don't rank high on the allergenic list may be capable of inducing allergic reactions in some people. Food allergies also manifest with different symptoms for different people and will vary in severity with each individual. Food allergies can be hereditary, so you should take your family history of food allergies into consideration when you begin to introduce solid foods to your little one. Always consult with a pediatrician when you introduce solid food to your baby.

You'll want to be especially careful with introducing foods that are common allergens. The top eight most highly allergenic foods are as follows:

- Dairy: This is the most common food allergy in babies and children under the age of 4; it's typically outgrown as the child ages.
  » Introduce at 6 months of age; yogurt only. When used in a recipe, milk is acceptable for babies, but it should not be given as a drink to babies until they are over the age of 12 months.

- Eggs: These are second to dairy as the most common food allergy in kids.
  » Introduce at 6 to 8 months

- Soy/soybeans
  » Introduce at 6 to 8 months

- Fish
  » Introduce at 8 months for light, white fish (such as cod and haddock) and salmon

- Crustaceans/shellfish
  » Introduce after 12 or 24 months depending on family history

- Wheat
  » Introduce at 6 to 8 months of age

- Peanuts: Research today is recommending that peanuts be introduced sooner rather than later.
  » Based on a landmark study published in 2015 called LEAP (Learning About Peanut Allergy), introducing peanut products around 6 months of age is now the recommendation. This recommendation became official in early 2017. It is still *very important* that you discuss peanut introduction with your baby's pediatrician and that you rely only on your physician's advice.

- Tree nuts

These eight foods are responsible for nearly 90 percent of all food allergies. Be aware that the recommended ages to introduce these foods to your baby are always being fine-tuned as scientific research continues to allow us to understand more and more about food allergies. Again, when introducing any new food to your infant, always consult with a pediatrician.

Common manifestations of an allergic reaction may include

- Vomiting

- Coughing

- Wheezing

- Red and/or watery eyes

- Hives

- Swelling of the face, mouth, or hands

- Anaphylaxis

Not all allergic reactions will present with the symptoms noted above, and allergic reactions can be immediate or take up to 2 hours to appear. In other cases, known as delayed food allergy reactions, symptoms don't appear for 6 to 8 hours. The American College of Allergy, Asthma, and Immunology notes "another type of delayed food allergy reaction stems from food protein-induced enterocolitis syndrome (FPIES), a severe gastrointestinal reaction that generally occurs 2 to 6 hours after consuming milk, soy, certain grains, and some other solid foods." FPIES most often occurs in infants who are being exposed to these foods for the first time or who are being weaned. It often involves repetitive vomiting, which can lead to dehydration, and in some cases bloody diarrhea. It is important to pay attention to any onset of vomiting and/or change in your baby's stools, especially if diarrhea begins to occur.

Finally, note that though the eight food groups mentioned are responsible for the vast majority of allergies, other foods—and even spices—can be triggers for certain people. For example, be aware that some babies can experience atopic reactions to cinnamon. These include rashes, itching, hives, and stomach pain.

Other Reactions or Signs of Intolerance

There are some foods that cause what may seem to be an allergic reaction when in fact the reaction may just be temporary or an intolerance due to the makeup and composition of the food itself.

Gassiness and bloating: Beans and legumes, along with cruciferous vegetables such as broccoli, brussels sprouts, and cauliflower, may cause babies to develop stomach pains and become very gassy; this happens with some adults, too. This gassiness is not due to an allergy. As baby gets older, the severity and occurrence of gassiness may subside.

Weird poop and other elimination oddities: Blueberries may cause babies to have grayish-colored poop, and when babies eliminate bananas, you may be surprised to see little tan or blackish particles that look like worms. Don't panic: These changes in poop are benign and don't mean that your baby is allergic or sick. It's also important to note that when you feed your baby asparagus, his urine may temporarily turn a greenish tinge and will be rather pungent in odor. Once the asparagus passes through his system, so too will the urine's color and smell.

Constipation: When babies first begin to eat solid foods, there will be many changes in their poop patterns, including a change in the composition and makeup of the stool itself. Firm or infrequent stools do not always mean that baby has a true case of constipation. One thing to understand is that constipation is not necessarily a result of a food allergy or intolerance, but it could be a result of feeding certain foods to your baby too often.

Bananas, applesauce, and rice are highly constipating. These foods have a high volume of soluble fiber that soaks up water/liquid and can cause hard stools. If your baby becomes constipated or has hard stools, you should cut down on feeding him these binding foods and instead offer foods that are high in fiber, such as peaches, pears, prunes, and plums. The "P" fruits will help to alleviate constipation. Barley and oatmeal will also help to get things moving again. Be sure to consult your baby's pediatrician if constipation lingers for more than 2 days.

Diarrhea: Call your pediatrician if your baby has a bout of diarrhea. In most instances, physicians should see babies who have diarrhea as soon as possible. It is very easy for a baby with diarrhea to become dehydrated. Babies seldom have diarrhea due to foods, but there are a few foods that can cause loose stools if fed on a continual basis. The "P" fruits that help to halt constipation can also cause overly loose stools. These runny and/or watery stools may not necessarily be diarrhea, but it's a good idea to pay close attention to your baby's diapers and call the doctor. Because babies can quickly dehydrate when they have diarrhea, scaling back their solid foods and offering just their milk feeds is a good idea until you have consulted with your pediatrician.

Rashes: Any food has the potential to cause baby to have diaper rash or other types of rashes. Citrus fruits may cause babies to have diaper rash and rashes around their mouths. These rashes are typically due to the high acidity of the fruit itself and often are not due to a true allergy to the citrus.

The Best Starter Foods and Why: Meats, Fruits, and Veggies

The foods that you choose to offer your baby as you introduce solids should be nutrient dense, single ingredient only, unseasoned, and easy to digest and swallow. Trying to figure out what foods to introduce and when can be very confusing. For example, why are sweet potatoes and bananas a great first food but corn and cauliflower are not? Why shouldn't we add herbs and spices right away?

To understand this, think about the "food" that baby has been eating from birth to 6 months of age. He has been eating nothing but a liquid diet of formula and/or breast milk. His digestive system is still sensitive and used to processing nothing but these liquids. Imagine how your baby's digestive system would react if his first meal of solid foods was a seasoned mix of a veggie, a meat, and a starch. His digestive system would have difficulty processing all of those different foods at once, and your baby would likely end up with terrible digestive issues and bowel troubles. Besides the possible digestive upsets, you would have no idea if baby has any food sensitivities or allergies.

Follow the 3-to-4-Day Wait Rule for a Happy Digestive System

This is where the 3-to-4-day wait rule comes into play. Introducing more than one new food at a time will make it difficult for you to determine which food is the culprit if your baby experiences any issues. Instead, introduce only one new food at a time and wait 3 to 4 days before introducing the next new food. This way, you can determine how the new food is affecting your baby. Follow the 3- to 4-day wait rule for at least the first 4 to 6 weeks of introducing solid foods. Once baby has tried a variety of foods, you can then begin to mix a few ingredients together that you know are safe and make combination meals.

Here's an example of how the 3- to 4-day waiting rule might play out:

- Days 1–3: apples

- Days 4–6: butternut squash

- Days 7–9: bananas

- Days 10–12: avocados

- Days 13–15: peaches

- Days 16–18: peas

Once a food has been introduced separately and hasn't presented any problems, you can continue to serve it as you introduce new foods. For instance, is this example, you can serve apples and butternut squash from days 1 through 6 while you're testing bananas during days 7 through 9. For more options, go to chapter 6.

Best Starter Foods at 4 to 6 Months of Age and Older

Fruits: apples, avocados, peaches, pears, bananas, plums

Vegetables: butternut (winter) squash, sweet potatoes, carrots

Meats and proteins: beef, chicken (not recommended under 6 months of age)

Grains: oatmeal, rice

The above foods are perfect starter foods over the course of the first month of introducing solid foods because they are

- Nutrient dense

- Easy to digest

- Easy to blend into a smooth texture

- Simple but great tasting and mostly loved by babies

Cereals and grains: Though cereals don't have to be the very first food that a baby eats, this has traditionally been the case. Nutritionally, there is no need to use a commercial cereal as baby's first food. However, if there are concerns about adequate iron and iron intake, you may be advised to begin with a fortified cereal. Grains that are not considered allergenic, such as rice, oatmeal, and barley, are typically introduced first. Wheat, an allergenic grain, is now introduced between 6 and 8 months of age or older depending on your family history of wheat allergies.

Fruits: Fruits are very good for babies because they offer lots of vitamin C and other important nutrients such as fiber. There are a few fruits such as strawberries, citrus, and even kiwifruit that can cause atopic dermatitis (rashes), and these are best to feed to your baby at a later age. Most fruits should be at least gently steamed when feeding as a beginner food. This will help the foods to be more easily digested. Bananas and avocados don't have to be cooked or steamed, and some foods such as peaches and pears may be easily mashed when raw.

Veggies: Vegetables are most flavorful when they are roasted or slow cooked. It's always wise to serve cooked veggies to your baby until she is at least 2 years of age. Ensure that she can chew well enough so that no choking hazard is present. Vegetables are not often allergenic but can cause other issues for young babies. Cruciferous vegetables such as broccoli, cauliflower, and brussels sprouts can cause discomforting gas, so it wouldn't be a good idea to introduce these as first foods. Other vegetables cause odd issues; asparagus, for example, can make baby's urine smell very off and turn a greenish tinge. Remember this when you first offer your baby this tasty little member of the lily family.

Meats, fish, and other proteins: Always serve meats, fish, and other forms of protein fully cooked. Meats and fish should not have pink areas and should *never* be fed to babies in their raw state.

Dairy: Do not replace breast milk or formula with milk of any type until after 12 months of age because serious health risks are possible. Don't give low-fat dairy products to a child under the age of 2 because most young children need these calories from fat for growth and brain development. Nut milks and milks made from grains such as rice, almond, cashew, coconut, and hemp are not nutritionally equivalent to dairy milk. These milks are low in fat, and most lack the nutritional profile that a growing baby or toddler needs. It is very important that you talk to your pediatrician and/or a certified registered dietician about giving your baby these milks.

Below are some simple sample charts that detail acceptable foods for each stage of your baby's development.

Stage One (a): 4 Months
Grains: rice, oatmeal
Fruits: apples, avocados, peaches, pears, bananas, plums
Vegetables: butternut (winter) squash, sweet potatoes, pumpkin
Dairy: None

Stage One (b): 6 to 8 Months
Grains and seeds: rice, oatmeal, barley, kamut, flax, quinoa
Fruits: apples, avocados, apricots, bananas, blueberries, cherries, cranberries, nectarines, pears, peaches, plums
Vegetables: butternut or any winter squash, carrots, green beans, sweet potatoes, peas, legumes (such as lentils, kidney beans, butter beans, etc.), parsnips, pumpkin, white potatoes, zucchini and summer squash
Dairy: yogurt, cottage cheese, cheese (no soft cheeses such as Brie until after 12 months)
Meats: egg yolk, chicken, beef, pork, salmon, cod, tofu

Stage Two: 8 to 10 Months
Grains: rice, oatmeal, barley, kamut, flax, wheat, pasta, amaranth, quinoa
Fruits: apples, avocados, bananas, blueberries, cherries, cranberries, mango, kiwifruit, nectarines, pear, peaches, plums
Vegetables: asparagus, beets, broccoli, butternut or any winter squash, cauliflower, carrots, corn, green beans, sweet potatoes, peas, legumes (such as lentils, kidney beans, butter beans, etc.), parsnips, white potatoes, spinach, kale and other leafy greens, zucchini and summer squash
Dairy: yogurt, cottage cheese, cheese (no soft cheeses such as Brie until after 12 months)
Meats/fish/protein: eggs, chicken, beef, pork, salmon, cod, tofu

Stage Three: 10 Months and Older
Grains and seeds: Any. Continue to watch for digestive upsets and allergic reactions.
Fruits: Any, including citrus and strawberries. Continue to watch for digestive upsets and allergic reactions.
Vegetables: Any, continue to watch for digestive upsets.
Dairy: yogurt, cottage cheese, sour cream, cheese (no soft cheeses such as Brie until after 12 months)
Meats/fish/protein: Any, but no shellfish or crustaceans until after 12 months of age or when your baby's pediatrician tells you that these are okay to feed to your baby.

Herbs, Spices, and Sweet and Savory Flavors—No Salt, No Sugar

Feeding babies solid foods can be nerve-racking with all of the "dos and don'ts" that there are to remember. But one of the most important "don'ts" is this: *Don't* add salt or sugar to the foods that you feed your baby. As adults, it can be and often is just automatic that we reach out and grab that saltshaker or the sugar bowl and proceed to shake and heap on the flavor. It may be tempting to do the same for baby's foods. But for the sake of baby's health, please refrain.

This doesn't mean, though, that baby food must be bland. If your baby is 6 months old or older and has been eating solid foods for 2 weeks or more without tummy trouble, you can begin flavoring your homemade baby food with herbs and spices, which add flavor without salt or sugar. Remember that your baby's palate is clean, and she will be able to learn to love the natural tastes of foods. For example, she has no idea that there are sweet flavored yogurts out there. Without the addition of sugar and other sweet ingredients, yogurt is naturally tart. Your baby will learn to love the taste of unsweetened yogurt because she will know nothing else. How amazing will it be that your baby learns to like the taste of foods in their natural state, without sweeteners and unhealthy additions?

Here are a few of the herbs and spices you can use to make your baby's food even more delicious:

Basil: savory; great with vegetables, sauces, pasta dishes, and soups

Cardamom: savory and sweet; great with fruits and in chicken and grain dishes

Cinnamon: sweet; add to oatmeal, pancakes, and vegetables and fruits such as carrots, pumpkin, cranberries, squash, and sweet potatoes; mix into yogurt and fruit sauces

Dill: savory; add to potatoes, chicken, and fish dishes; and when roasted, use it on vegetables including carrots and cauliflower

Garlic: savory; garlic is great with any vegetable dish and goes well with sautéed greens and in meatballs, savory sauces, and roasted meats

Ginger: savory and sweet; sprinkle ginger on pears or carrots and then slow-cook or roast them. Add fresh grated ginger to grain dishes, soups, and chicken dishes, too.

Mint: sweet; mint makes a great addition to pureed peas and yogurt blends

Nutmeg: sweet or savory; add nutmeg to roasted root vegetables, any type of winter squash dish, or fruit sauce such as applesauce or pear sauce

Oregano: savory; use oregano in chicken and turkey dishes, soups, and sauces

Pepper: savory; pepper is a great addition to any meat or vegetable dish

Rosemary: savory; this little herb is a fantastic addition to chicken, pork, and roasted or slow-cooked vegetables

Sage: savory; use sage for poultry dishes and winter squash and root vegetables; add it to chicken soup and chicken pot pie, too

Thyme: savory; another spice that's nice with poultry and root vegetables and in stocks, soups, and broths

Turmeric: savory; a yellow herb that adds a bit of a warm flavor to chicken, beef, and fish or can be used with root vegetables and in marinades

Vanilla: sweet; use vanilla in all fruit sauces and as a great addition to flavor yogurt and cranberry sauce

Feeding Baby: Let the Fun Begin!

Now that you know *what* to feed baby, let's talk a little bit about the actual feeding process. This is the fun part of baby food—and also the potentially frustrating part. Here are a few things to know as you begin this wild, crazy, and fulfilling journey.

Spoon-Feeding vs. Baby-Led Weaning or Self-Feeding

The debate about whether you should use the puree with spoon-feeding method or the baby-led/self-feeding method to introduce solid foods continues to grow and to divide parents. Both methods have benefits and drawbacks, but no matter which you choose, it's important to focus on one thing: you are feeding and nourishing your baby and teaching her healthy eating habits early. In the years to come, it isn't going to matter if her first bites were from a spoon or from smears and smashed bits of foods on her high chair tray. What will matter is that she has learned to enjoy a wide variety of fresh and wholesome foods without relying on added sugars or salt.

> Until the age of ten to twelve months, always nurse or give baby a formula bottle before you offer solid foods. Breast milk and/or formula are the most important sources of nutrition for growing babies until they're ten to twelve months old.

The spoon: If you choose to spoon-feed your baby, the most important thing you should do is learn to pay attention to baby's signals. If your baby begins to turn away from the spoon, that shows you she has had enough. You should stop feeding her and respect her cues. A baby's tummy is about the size of her fist. Babies know when they are full, and with such little tummies, they don't need a lot to fill up. By respecting her cues, you'll help her to learn how to regulate her food intake and understand when she's full. Resist the urge for "just one more bite."

Baby-led weaning or self-feeding: If you are going to try the baby-led/self-feeding method, be certain that your baby's pincer grasp is well developed so that he can pick up or scoop up the foods. Ensure that all foods you offer are easy to mash between the gums. Baby's gums are very strong but cannot mash foods if those foods aren't soft enough. You can test out the softness of a food by either squishing it gently between your thumb and forefinger or by trying to swirl and break it up in your mouth. With baby-led weaning or self-feeding, you may think that the small bit of avocado and mashed banana your baby eats isn't enough to satisfy or nourish him, but remember that his stomach is only the size of his fist and also keep in mind that he has eaten his regular milk feeding. When baby lets you know that he is finished, you can be 99.9 percent certain that he truly is.

How Your Baby Says "I'm Full"

Watch for these signs that your baby has had enough food and you should end the feeding:

Closed mouth: When the spoon comes close, your baby may close her mouth and shake her head. This could also be a sign that your baby doesn't like a food you have given her, but when this is the case, her face will tell you "yuck."

Back at you: If you have fed a few spoonfuls or have tried to put another bit of food into baby's mouth and he spits it out, he's probably full. You have the next meal to look forward to.

Turning away: When baby starts turning her head away as the spoon comes closer, she's letting you know that she is full or just doesn't want to eat anymore. Respect that and know that she won't starve because she didn't eat that last bite.

How Much, How Often

When you first start feeding baby solid foods, do it in the morning or the afternoon and after the regular nursing or formula feeding. This way, if your baby has any type of reaction, she won't be up all night with a painful tummy or bout of hives, and you will be able to get to a doctor's office, if needed.

Babies starting solid foods eat a very small amount of solids, usually just ½ tablespoon or a small smear of food on a tray. Again, remember that baby's tummy is about the size of his fist. If you begin to fret that your baby isn't eating enough solid foods, look at his fist to remind yourself that it doesn't take much to fill him up. By the time babies are 10 to 12 months old, they will be eating larger portions and relying more on solid foods for their nutrition.

Starters (4 to 6 Months)

Breakfast or early lunch: 1 tablespoon of a single fruit or vegetable in the morning or the afternoon; add 1 tablespoon of cereal after a week. Remember that your baby may not even eat the full tablespoon; this is okay!

Intermediates (6 to 8 Months)

Breakfast: 1 to 2 tablespoons of a fruit or veggie; 1 to 2 tablespoons of yogurt, egg yolk, a grain, or meat

Lunch: 1 to 2 tablespoons of a fruit or veggie; 1 to 2 tablespoons of yogurt, egg yolk, a grain, or meat

Dinner: 1 to 2 tablespoons of a fruit or veggie; 1 to 2 tablespoons of yogurt, egg yolk, a grain, or meat

Experienced (8 to 12 Months)

Around 8 to 9 months of age, many babies will be eating three meals of solid foods a day. At this age, your baby's appetite will continue to change from one meal to the next, so don't worry if your baby isn't eating three full meals each and every day. Keep serving iron-rich foods to help maintain baby's iron stores and foods with vitamin C to aid iron absorption. Make creative combinations of foods including meats, fruits, and vegetables and also yogurt and/or cheese. Not all of these foods need to be fed at one sitting, but try to rotate them throughout the meals of the day.

Breakfast: Combinations of fruits, vegetables, yogurt, eggs, grains, and meats

Lunch: Combinations of fruits, vegetables, yogurt, eggs, grains, and meats

Dinner: Combinations of fruits, vegetables, yogurt, eggs, grains, and meats

PART TWO
Let's Get Slow Cooking!

First Foods:
Great Single-Ingredient Dishes

Beginning the transition of weaning your baby from a diet of only breast milk and/or formula to a varied diet of solid foods is a huge milestone. Congratulations! When you're first starting this process, single-ingredient meals are best. Remember that up until now, your baby's digestive system has handled only liquids, so starting out slowly with one food at a time helps your baby's system make this transition more smoothly. Also, by sticking to single-ingredient meals and waiting 3 to 4 days before introducing each new food, you'll be able to more easily identify the cause of allergic or digestive reactions to a food. Please note that none of the recipes in this chapter contain foods that are considered to be allergenic. However, you should always work with your pediatrician when introducing new foods to your baby.

Single ingredients may not seem exciting, but this doesn't mean your baby will be eating bland and boring foods. Remember, your baby has no notion of bland and boring at this stage. While you may think that a meal of pureed carrots isn't exciting, your baby's clean palate and taste buds will be delighted with the new taste of carrots and with every new taste and texture that comes on a spoon or is plopped on a tray. It's also important to have kids become accustomed to individual flavors so that they will learn to love each food as it is, in all its delicious and healthy glory. Once your baby has had a few single-ingredient meals, then you can start to combine and mix those foods together to create new flavors and textures. This initial "stage one" experience will be far from bland and boring, you'll see!

A note about water: You may notice the addition of water in many of the following single-ingredient fruit recipes. Traditionally, sugar is used in recipes because it helps fruits to break down and helps to release natural juices within the fruits. This is why you have juicy apples for pie filling when you combine sugar with peeled and chopped apples. Because we are cooking the following recipes for beginning eaters, however, we absolutely want to avoid the use of sugar. Instead, I add water to help our fruits cook down nice and soft.

A note about adding fats: Fats such as olive oil, coconut oil, and even real butter are good for growing babies. A baby's brain needs lots of fat to develop properly, so don't shy away from adding a bit of any of the mentioned fats when cooking for baby.

Slow Cooker Apples

Using a slow cooker to create a wide variety of apple dishes is a big tradition in my house, especially during the fall. The smell of apples and spices cooking fills the house with deliciousness and makes everyone happy. Sometimes, it truly is the little things that make my family happy. Enjoy the wonderful warmth of apples in the slow cooker.

Age and Stage: 6 months+ | Stage One | First Foods and Beyond

Slow Cooker Size: 4 to 6 quarts (3.8 to 5.7 l)

3 pounds (1.4 kg) sweet, not too sour, apples, such as McIntosh, Gala, or Fuji
1 cup (235 ml) cold water
Dash of ground cinnamon or nutmeg (optional)

1. Core and peel the apples. Using an apple slicer, slice the apples.
2. Combine the apple slices and water in the slow cooker. If your baby is 8 months old or older, add the cinnamon or nutmeg.
3. Cover and cook on low for 4 to 6 hours, or until the apples have been reduced to a sauce.
4. Remove the apples from the slow cooker and set aside to cool.

Preparation and Storage for Baby

If the texture is appropriate for your baby straight from the slow cooker, set aside a portion or two for baby's meal. Otherwise, place the cooled apples in a blender or food processor and process to a texture that is appropriate for your baby. Add water, formula, or breast milk as needed.

Store in the refrigerator for up to 3 days for babies.

To freeze, follow the stage one directions for beginner eaters in "Freezing Homemade Baby Food" on page 28.

For the Family

To make a quick and tasty applesauce, set aside a portion for the family and add some cinnamon or nutmeg, if you haven't already done so. Try dipping sliced avocados or bananas into the applesauce for a tasty snack.

❄ Freezes well, but color may change.   🍎 Vitamins A, C, and E, potassium, calcium, and magnesium

Easy Apricots

If you've never cooked apricots into a jam or a sauce, you will be surprised at how sticky these little fruits are as they simmer. If you plop some of this tasty puree down on baby's tray, you'll be able to see the curiosity as baby feels this new texture.

Age and Stage: 6 months+ | Stage One | First Foods and Beyond
Slow Cooker Size: 4 quarts (3.8 l)

1½ pounds (680 g) dried apricots (unsulfured)
2½ cups (570 ml) cold water
Dash of vanilla extract or pinch of ground ginger (optional)

1. Place the apricots in the slow cooker and cover with the water.
2. If your baby is 8 months old or older, add the vanilla or ginger. Stir to combine.
3. Cover and cook on low for 4 to 6 hours, stirring after the first hour, or until the apricots have been reduced to a thick sauce. (They will be rather thick and sticky.) Remove from the slow cooker and set aside to cool.

Preparation and Storage for Baby

If the texture is appropriate for your baby straight from the slow cooker, set aside a portion or two for baby's meal and feed after the apricots have cooled. Otherwise, place the cooled apricots into a blender or food processor and process to a texture that is appropriate for your baby. Pureeing apricots can be tricky due to the texture, so you will probably have to add water, formula, or breast milk to reduce them to a thin puree for beginner eaters.

Store in the refrigerator for up to 3 days for babies.

To freeze, follow the stage one directions in "Freezing Homemade Baby Food" on page 28. Note that apricot sauce won't freeze solid but will remain a bit tacky and sticky.

For the Family

Set aside a portion of apricots to add to any chicken or pork dish or mix into breakfast cereals. You can also add additional vanilla to the apricot puree to give it more flavor. Apricot puree can easily be turned into a jam to spread over toast or muffins. Or try creating an apricot marinade using 1 cup pureed apricots, ½ cup soy sauce, a squeeze of lemon, 1 tablespoon minced garlic, and 1 cup extra-virgin olive oil. Whisk all ingredients together and marinate chicken breasts or pork chops for the family.

Apricots are great for helping to ease constipation. They can also be used as a thickening ingredient in recipes.

Of all foods, apricots contain the highest levels of carotenoids, antioxidants that give the apricots their orange color and help protect the body's cells and skin and eyes.

❄ Freezes well, but may be sticky or tacky in texture. 🍎 Vitamins A and C, iron, potassium, copper, fiber

Cherries Hooray

My kids were never big fans of cherries. They were, however, big fans of smooshing and swirling and finger painting with cherry sauce. Now that they're older, they love cherries and especially spitting out the pits, which we try to keep to a minimum. Remember, a little food play is a good thing (repeat this three times and don't forget to breathe!). Serve cherry and blueberry together and you may just wind up with purple sauce!

Age and Stage: 6 months+ | Stage One | First Foods and Beyond
Slow Cooker Size: 4 to 6 quarts (3.8 to 5.7 l); oval

3 pounds (1.4 kg) fresh cherries or 3 bags (1 pound [455 g] each) frozen cherries
3 cups (710 ml) cold water (or a combination of apple juice and water to give the cherry sauce a less sour taste)

1. If using fresh cherries, rinse the cherries. Pit and remove the stems. Rinse again. (See sidebar if you don't want to take the time to hand pit each cherry.)
2. Place the rinsed or frozen cherries in the slow cooker. Add the water and stir to combine.
3. Cover and cook on low for 4 to 6 hours. Check after about 2 hours and stir or remove the cherries to pit (see sidebar). The cherries will be bubbly and maybe even frothy, but don't be alarmed. Allow them to cook for 2 to 3 hours longer or until reduced to a nice sauce. Remove the cherries from the slow cooker and set aside to cool. When the cherries have cooled, you may wish to run them through a strainer to remove any skins.

Preparation and Storage for Baby

If the texture is appropriate for your baby straight from the slow cooker, set aside a portion or two for baby's meal and feed after the cherries have cooled. Otherwise, blend or process the cherries to a texture that is appropriate for your baby. It is easiest to puree cherries using a handheld blender and blending right in the slow cooker. You may need to add water, formula, or breast milk to thin for beginner eaters.

The skins of the cherries will not completely disappear once the cherries have been pureed; however, the tiny bits of skin should not be a choking issue.

Store in the refrigerator for up to 3 days for babies.

To freeze, follow the stage one directions for beginner eaters in "Freezing Homemade Baby Food" on page 28.

> *For this recipe, there are two methods to pit the cherries. To pit them individually, insert the tip of a vegetable peeler in the stem end of the fruit, rotate around the pit, and scoop it out. Alternately, place the stemmed cherries (with their pits) in the slow cooker. After 2 hours of cooking, remove the cherries and allow to cool briefly. Transfer the cherries to a strainer and push them through into a bowl. The pits will be left behind. Return the strained cherries to the slow cooker and continue to cook for 3 to 4 hours longer.*

For the Family

With the remainder of the cherry sauce, you may wish to add a bit of vanilla and, if desired, a small amount of ground cinnamon and honey or sugar. You can put the sauce back into the slow cooker and cook it longer so that it thickens to a jam. The sauce is great mixed into oatmeal, spread on warm corn bread, or added to plain yogurt.

❄ Freezes well.   🍎 Vitamins A, C, K, and folate, too!

Blueberries for Compote or Puree

Blueberry puree will really make a mess out of your baby's clothing and hands, as well as the high chair tray, the floor, any clothing you're wearing, and whatever else it comes into contact with! Don't let this stop you from letting your baby explore the puree with her hands. Playing with food helps teach babies about texture and lets them know that mealtimes should be fun. And if you don't have twins, like I do, you'll have only a single mess to clean up! Happy playing.

Age and Stage: 6 months+ | Stage One | First Foods and Beyond
Slow Cooker Size: 4 to 6 quarts (3.8 to 5.7 l); oval

4 quarts (2.32 kg) fresh blueberries or 3 bags (1 pound [455 g] each) frozen blueberries
¼ to ½ cup (60 to 120 ml) cold water

1. Rinse the blueberries, if using fresh. Place the blueberries in the slow cooker. If using fresh berries, add ½ cup (120 ml) of water. If using frozen berries, add ¼ cup (60 ml) of water. Stir to combine.
2. Cover and cook on low for 4 to 6 hours. Check after about 2 hours and stir. The blueberries will be bubbly, and maybe even frothy, but don't be concerned. Once the blueberries have been reduced to a sauce, remove them from the slow cooker and set them aside to cool.

Preparation and Storage for Baby

If the texture is appropriate for your baby straight from the slow cooker, set aside a portion or two for baby's meal and feed after the blueberries have cooled. Otherwise, place the blueberries into a blender or food processor and process to a texture that is appropriate for your baby. If needed for beginner eaters, add water, formula, or breast milk to thin, but the mixture will likely be thin enough for most babies.

The skins of the blueberries will not completely disappear once pureed; however, the tiny bits of skin should not be a choking issue.

Store in the refrigerator for up to 3 days for babies.

To freeze, follow the stage one directions for beginner eaters in "Freezing Homemade Baby Food" on page 28.

> *After your baby has eaten blueberries, you may be surprised to find that her stool is grayish and contains little black flecks (the blueberry skins). Don't be alarmed—this happens to many babies who eat blueberry puree!*
>
> *Of course, you should always talk to your pediatrician whenever you notice changes in bowel movements and cannot link the change to any food or health event.*

For the Family

Set aside a portion of the blueberry sauce and add a bit of lemon, ground cinnamon, and vanilla. If desired, you could also add a small amount of honey or sugar. You can mix the sauce into oatmeal or breakfast cereals or add it to plain yogurt.

❄ Freezes well. 🍎 Vitamins A, C, and folate, plus fiber! Blueberries are also high in antioxidants and may help reduce cholesterol in people of all ages.

Cranberries: Not Just for the Holidays!

Cranberries are also known as bounce berries. Tradition says that long ago, people used to toss cranberries down the stairs (this is likely a myth, I would hope) or drop them to see if they bounced. The bouncing berries were ripe, and they were the ones to use. Don't tell your kids about this, though; they'll wear you down until you give in and let them toss some cranberries down the stairs. If you do get worn down, use the outside deck stairs to avoid a mess in the house. Trust me on this one!

Age and Stage: 6 months+ | Stage One | First Foods and Beyond
Slow Cooker Size: 4 to 6 quarts (3.8 to 5.7 l); round and deep

Raw cranberries freeze incredibly well. Simply toss the bag in the freezer. I have found that they maintain freshness for up to 9 months. You can cook them on the stovetop or in the slow cooker without having to thaw them first.

3 bags (12 ounces [340 g] each) fresh cranberries
3 cups (710 ml) cold water or 2 cups (475 ml) water and 1 cup (235 ml) apple juice (always use only 100 percent real fruit juice that's free of high-fructose corn syrup)
1 teaspoon vanilla extract (optional)
½ teaspoon ground nutmeg (optional)

1. Rinse the cranberries and place in the slow cooker. Pour the water or water and juice over the cranberries and stir to combine. If baby is over 8 months old, add the vanilla and nutmeg.
2. Cover and cook on low for about 4 hours, stirring at least once an hour. When all of the cranberries have popped, remove them from the slow cooker and set aside to cool. You can either leave them as is or mash them in a bowl. (I like to use a potato masher to mash them up a bit and then let them simmer for another 30 minutes.)

Preparation and Storage for Baby

The texture of the cooked cranberries straight out of the slow cooker will likely not be good for your baby, so place the cooled cranberries in a blender or food processor and process them to a texture that is appropriate for your baby. You can also puree the cranberries using a handheld blender and blending right in the slow cooker. You may need to add water to create a smoother puree; you will not get cranberries to puree into a 100 percent smooth texture. You can also use formula or breast milk to thin for beginner eaters.

The skins of the cranberries will not completely disappear once they have been pureed; however, the tiny bits of skin should not be a choking issue.

Store in the refrigerator for up to 3 days for babies.

To freeze, follow the stage one directions for beginner eaters in "Freezing Homemade Baby Food" on page 28.

For the Family

If you haven't flavored or spiced the cranberries during cooking, add the cranberries to a saucepan and heat until just bubbling. Once bubbling, add 2 teaspoons of vanilla extract and, if desired, 1 teaspoon of ground cinnamon and ½ cup (115 g) of packed brown sugar. You can also return the sauce to the slow cooker and cook it longer so that it thickens to a jam. The sauce is great for the holidays, of course, but it's also delicious when mixed in with chicken salad, smoothies, and oatmeal. Or mix it into plain yogurt and spread on toasted bread.

❄ Freezes well, but may not freeze completely solid.　🍎 Vitamins C, E, and K, plus copper and fiber

Peaches, Peaches, Peaches

Diced peaches make great finger foods for little ones but can be very slippery. Watching your baby chase diced peaches around her tray may seem cruel, but she is learning valuable fine-motor skills. I used to crush up Cheerios or other oat or corn cereals and then use the crumbs or dust to coat the bits of foods. The coating makes them much easier to pick up!

Age and Stage: 6 months+ | Stage One | First Foods and Beyond
Slow Cooker Size: 4 to 6 quarts (3.8 to 5.7 l); oval

Babies who start solid foods may become a bit "bound up" and have difficulty pooping. Peaches are a natural laxative and will help to get things moving properly again!

If you can't wait for the slow cooker peaches, you can always mash up very ripe raw peaches or steam them on the stovetop. Please watch out for the skins before feeding to your baby!

3 pounds (1.4 kg) fresh peaches or 1 bag (2 pounds [907 g]) frozen sliced peaches
½ to 1 cup (120 to 235 ml) water
1 teaspoon vanilla extract (optional)
½ teaspoon ground cinnamon (optional)

1. If using fresh peaches, wash them well, cut in half, and remove the pits. If desired, peel. Chop into quarters. Place the fresh or frozen peaches in the slow cooker.
2. If baby is over 8 months old, add the vanilla and cinnamon.
3. Cover and cook on low for 3 to 4 hours, stirring after 1 hour. Frozen peaches will simmer down faster than fresh peaches. Once they've reached a nice saucy consistency, remove them from the slow cooker and set aside to cool. If you left the skin on, you will have to puree the peaches unless you can mash them so that no larger bits of skin are in the sauce. Babies can handle the skins of soft fruits, but the skins must be small enough so that they don't pose a choking hazard.

Preparation and Storage for Baby

Place the cooled peaches in a blender or food processor and process to a texture that is appropriate for your baby; please be mindful of the size of the peach skin pieces. Alternately, you can puree the peaches using a handheld blender and blending right in the slow cooker. You may need to add water, formula, or breast milk to create a smooth puree.

The skins of the peaches will not completely disappear once they have been pureed; however, the tiny bits of skin should not be a choking issue. Don't be surprised if you see little bits of peach skin in your baby's diaper.

Store in the refrigerator for up to 3 days for babies.

To freeze, follow the stage one directions for beginner eaters in "Freezing Homemade Baby Food" on page 28.

For the Family

You may wonder what you're going to do with all that peach sauce. Well, fill up some small Mason jars and give them as gifts. Or put the sauce back into the slow cooker and add some applesauce, additional vanilla, ginger, and nutmeg, and then simmer until the mix thickens to a jam. You could also mix the peach sauce with a bit of olive oil and spread on chicken prior to roasting or baking. Or mix the peaches into any winter squash side dish for a new flavor twist. And, of course, the old standbys are mixing with oatmeal, spreading on toast, or adding to plain yogurt.

❄ Freezes well, but may not freeze solid. 🍎 Vitamins A and C, fiber, and potassium

Pears—Nothing but Pears

Like peaches, pear dices make great finger foods for babies, even though they are slippery little fruits. My kids loved to smash the pear dices into the tray and then push the mess toward them. I'm still not sure why they did this, but I suspect it was due to the ease in which they could turn a pear dice into mush.

Age and Stage: 6 months+ | Stage One | First Foods and Beyond
Slow Cooker Size: 4 to 6 quarts (3.8 to 5.7 l); oval

3 pounds (1.4 kg) fresh pears
1 teaspoon vanilla extract (optional)
¼ teaspoon ground ginger (optional)

1. Wash, halve, and core the pears. If desired, peel. Chop into quarters and transfer to the slow cooker.
2. If baby is over 8 months old, add the vanilla and ginger.
3. Cover and cook on low for 3 hours, stirring after 1 hour. Pears will simmer down rather quickly (far more quickly than your kids when it's bedtime!). Once they've reached a nice saucy consistency, remove them from the slow cooker and set aside to cool. If you left the skin on, you will have to puree the pears unless you're able to remove the skins with a slotted spoon. Be sure to mash or puree so that no larger bits of skin are in the sauce. Babies can handle the skins of soft fruits, but the skins must be small enough so that they don't pose a choking hazard.

Preparation and Storage for Baby

Place the cooled pears in a blender or food processor and process to a texture that is appropriate for your baby; please be mindful of the size of the pear skin pieces. Alternately, you can puree the pears using a handheld blender and blending right in the slow cooker. You probably won't need to add water, formula, or breast milk to create a smooth puree.

The skins of the pears may not completely disappear once they have been pureed; however, the tiny bits of skin should not be a choking issue.

Store in the refrigerator for up to 3 days for babies.

To freeze, follow the stage one directions for beginner eaters in "Freezing Homemade Baby Food" on page 28.

For the Family

Use up extra sauce by putting it in small Mason jars and giving them to friends and family as gifts. You could also put the sauce back into the slow cooker and add some peach sauce, additional vanilla, cinnamon, and nutmeg and then simmer until the mix thickens to a jam. Pear puree is also very tasty in any winter squash side dish and even with chicken. Or follow the old standbys: mix into oatmeal, spread on toast, add to plain yogurt or smoothies, or even warm and spoon over vanilla ice cream.

※ Freezes well, but you may see ice crystal buildup due to the watery consistency of pears.
🍎 Vitamins B$_6$ and C, fiber, iron, and some calcium, too!

Plums: Keeping Up with the "P" Fruits

Plums were a difficult sell to my babies. I'm not going to lie, plum sauce without added sweetener or spices, or even just a bit of apple juice, tends to be tart and a bit sour, no matter how ripe the plums are. If you find your baby just won't eat plum sauce, you can mix it with pears or apples and then gradually cut down on the mix-in ration until, *voilà!*, baby is eating plain plum sauce.

Age and Stage: 6 months+ | Stage One | First Foods and Beyond
Slow Cooker Size: 4 to 6 quarts (3.8 to 5.7 l); oval

Like peaches and pears, plums are a natural laxative and will help to get things moving properly again.

3 pounds (1.4 kg) fresh plums
½ cup (120 ml) water or combination of ¼ cup (60 ml) apple juice and ¼ cup (60 ml) water
1 teaspoon vanilla extract (optional)

1. Wash, halve, and pit the plums. If desired, remove the peel. Chop the plums into quarters and transfer to the slow cooker.
2. Add the water or a combination of water and apple juice. If baby is over 8 months old, add the vanilla, if desired. Stir to combine.
3. Cover and cook on low for 3 hours, stirring after the first hour. Plums will simmer down quickly, so you may need only 2 hours of cook time. Once the plums have reached a nice saucy consistency, remove them from the slow cooker and set aside to cool. If you have left the skin on, you will have to puree the plums unless you want to remove the skins from the slow cooker bowl with a slotted spoon. Be sure to mash or puree so that no larger bits of skin are in the sauce. Babies can handle the skins of soft fruits, but the skins must be small enough so that they don't pose a choking hazard.

Preparation and Storage for Baby

Place the cooled plums in a blender or food processor and process to a texture that is appropriate for your baby; please be mindful of the size of the plum skin pieces. Alternately, you can puree the plums using a handheld blender and blending right in the slow cooker. You will probably not need to add water to create a smooth puree.

As with other fruits that have skins on, the skins of the plums may not completely disappear once they have been pureed; however, the tiny bits of skin should not be a choking issue.

Store in the refrigerator for up to 3 days for babies.

To freeze, follow the stage one directions for beginner eaters in "Freezing Homemade Baby Food" on page 28.

For the Family

If you'd like to gift your leftover plum sauce, resimmer the plums with pears or peaches or even apples and add some maple syrup, cinnamon, and vanilla. Be sure to simmer until the mixture thickens to a jam. Plum sauce can be good with chicken and pork dishes, and you could add it to smoothies or your warm breakfast cereal.

❊ Freezes well, but you may see ice crystal buildup due to the watery consistency of plums.
🍎 Vitamins C and K, fiber, potassium, iron, and copper, too!

Beans, Beans, They're Good for Your Everything!

Beans such as kidney, cannellini, black, and northern are great finger and baby-led weaning foods for little ones. When my boys had the pincer grasp and the sweeping motion down, they practiced the fine art of almost-throwing beans around. The dog was always happy with each new food milestone the boys passed.

Age and Stage: 6 months+ | Stage One | First Foods and Beyond
Slow Cooker Size: 4 to 6 quarts (3.8 to 5.7 l); deep or oval

1 bag (1 pound [455 g]) dried red kidney beans
6 cups (1.4 l) cold water
¼ cup (40 g) minced onion (optional)
¼ teaspoon ground black pepper (optional)

1. Place the beans in a bowl, cover with water, and soak for at least 5 hours.
2. Drain the beans, transfer to a saucepan, cover with water, and boil for 10 minutes.
3. Drain and rinse the boiled beans. Transfer to the slow cooker. Cover with the water. If baby is over 8 months old, add the onion and pepper.
4. Cover and cook on high for at least 6 hours, checking often. You may want to remove some of the beans when they are soft and set aside for the adult meal.

Preparation and Storage for Baby

The beans may soften enough that you can feed them to your baby straight from the slow cooker. If so, set aside a portion or two to cool for baby's meal. Otherwise, place the beans in a blender or food processor and process to a texture that is appropriate for your baby. Add water, formula, or breast milk as desired to create a thin puree.

Store in the refrigerator for up to 3 days for babies.

To freeze, follow the stage one directions for beginner eaters in "Freezing Homemade Baby Food" on page 28.

For the Family

Now that you have a nice bean puree, why not make hummus? Add some tahini and olive oil along with herbs and spices such as garlic (minced or powdered), pepper, and sriracha seasoning blend.

> **Caution:** *Beans must be soaked for at least 5 hours and then boiled for 10 minutes prior to cooking them in a slow cooker. These legumes will concentrate and emit phytohaemagglutinin, which is a form of lectin that can be toxic at high levels. Though it's present in many varieties of beans, it's highly concentrated in red kidney beans. Soaking and boiling beans prior to slow cooking will stop this potential health hazard from occurring. Note that white kidney beans contain less phytohaemagglutinin than red ones.*

❄ Freezes well.   🍎 B vitamins, including folate, and a bit of C, plus iron, calcium, and fiber

Beets: Eat Them, Color with Them

If you have ever peeled beets, you know how they stain your hands a red-pink color. When your babies are eating finger foods and you offer them diced beets, show them the color on their hands and watch the marvel in their eyes!

Age and Stage: 7 to 8 months+ | Stage One | First Foods and Beyond
Slow Cooker Size: 2 to 4 quarts (1.9 to 3.8 l); oval

> 2 pounds (907 g) beets
> ¼ cup (60 ml) cold water
> Pat of butter (optional)
> ¼ teaspoon poultry seasoning (optional)

1. Wash, peel, and roughly chop the beets. Transfer to the slow cooker and add the water.
2. If baby is over 8 months old, add the butter and poultry seasoning.
3. Cover and cook on low heat for 6 hours or until the beets are soft and caramelized.

Preparation and Storage for Baby

Place the cooled beets in a blender or food processor and process to a texture that is appropriate for your baby. Add water, formula, or breast milk as desired to create a thin puree.

Store in the refrigerator for up to 3 days for babies.

To freeze, follow the stage one directions for beginner eaters in "Freezing Homemade Baby Food" on page 28.

For the Family

Add some of the beet puree to cooked beans (see Beans, Beans, They're Good for Your Everything! on page 57) and make a pink hummus. Or put the beets on a baking sheet, drizzle with olive oil, sprinkle with sea salt and pepper, and then roast at 400°F (200°C) for 20 minutes.

❄ Freezes well. 🍎 B vitamins, including folate, and A and C, plus iron, calcium, and fiber

Broccoli: The Edible Green Tree

Broccoli makes a great puree and also a great finger food. When your baby is eating cheese, soft-cook the broccoli and let baby dunk the broccoli in grated cheese.

My boys would look at the florets for what seemed like hours and enjoyed eating broccoli soft-cooked far more than they liked it pureed.

Age and Stage: 7 to 8 months+ | Stage One | First Foods and Beyond
Slow Cooker Size: 4 to 6 quarts (3.8 to 5.7 l); deep or oval

3 pounds (1.4 kg) fresh broccoli
¾ cup (175 ml) water

1. Wash and then cut the broccoli florets from the stems. Chop the stems. Transfer the florets and stems to the slow cooker and add the water.
2. Cover and cook on low for 2 to 3 hours. You may want to remove some of the broccoli sooner if you prefer al dente broccoli for the big kids. Broccoli florets will cook and soften to mush that is great for babies, but the stems may not become as soft. Be sure to check the texture of the cooked broccoli stems before you serve to baby. You may need to puree the broccoli if your baby isn't eating textured foods yet. If she is enjoying texture and finger foods, lightly mash the stems with the florets if needed and serve.

Preparation and Storage for Baby

If the texture is appropriate for your baby straight from the slow cooker, set aside a portion or two for baby's meal. Otherwise, place the broccoli in a blender or food processor and process to a texture that is appropriate for your baby. Add water, formula, or breast milk as desired to create a thin puree.

Store in the refrigerator for up to 3 days for babies.

To freeze, follow the stage one directions for beginner eaters in "Freezing Homemade Baby Food" on page 28.

For the Family

Broccoli mush is not very appealing for us big kids, so don't forget to remove some of the broccoli from the slow cooker prior to the mush stage. One of the yummy things you can make if you slow-cook a lot of broccoli is a quick cheesy broccoli casserole.

4 cups (240 g) cooked broccoli
1 cup (120 g) grated cheddar cheese
¼ cup (55 g) butter, melted
½ cup (36 g) crushed crackers of your choice

1. Preheat the oven to 350°F (180°C).
2. In a bowl, combine the broccoli, cheese, butter, and crackers. Transfer to a greased shallow casserole dish.
3. Bake for 30 minutes or until bubbly.

> **Caution:** *Broccoli can cause tummy upset as well as gas. It is better to wait to serve broccoli to your baby until he is around 7 to 8 months of age.*

❄ Freezes well, if pureed, but does not freeze well as is.
🍎 B vitamins, including folate, and A, a lot of C, and K, as well as fiber, calcium, and iron

Diced Butternut or Acorn Squash

Butternut and acorn squash were much loved by all three of my boys. Whenever I cook it, I think of my grandma, who always had butternut or acorn squash at the Sunday dinner table, no matter what the season was. Food is not just to nourish the body—it can help nourish the soul, too!

Age and Stage: 6 months+ | Stage One | First Foods and Beyond
Slow Cooker Size: 4 to 6 quarts (3.8 to 5.7 l); deep or oval

2 pounds (907 g) fresh acorn or butternut squash
2 cups (475 ml) cold water

1. Wash and halve the squash. Remove the seeds and peel away the shell. Dice the flesh. Transfer the diced squash to the slow cooker and add the water.
2. Cover and cook on low for 6 hours. Check after about 3 hours and add more water if needed. The squash will simmer down to a very smooth texture as it cooks, so you may not need to puree it for your baby. If so, set aside a portion or two for baby's meal and feed after the squash has cooled.

Preparation and Storage for Baby

If necessary, place the squash in a blender or food processor and process to a texture that is appropriate for your baby. Add water, formula, or breast milk as desired to create a thin puree.

Store in the refrigerator for up to 3 days for babies.

To freeze, follow the stage one directions for beginner eaters in "Freezing Homemade Baby Food" on page 28.

For the Family

Add butter, ground cinnamon, and a bit of vanilla to the extra squash for a tasty side dish that goes well with any entrée. If soup's on your mind, take out a saucepan and add 3 cups (710 ml) of chicken or vegetable broth and 1½ cups (380 g) of cooked squash. Whisk together and warm on the stovetop. Dish out squash soup and top individual servings with a dollop of sour cream.

These winter squash varieties are true favorites of babies everywhere. Their smooth texture and mild flavor make this squash a great first food choice. Plus, they are loaded with vitamin A and are incredibly healthy.

❄ Freezes well, but may be watery when thawed; mix to recombine
● Vitamins A, C, and E, plus iron, potassium, calcium, and magnesium

Whole Butternut or Acorn Squash—Just Toss It In!

Okay, you are going to read this recipe and think one of two things: Either this lady is totally insane, or this lady is the most clever person to walk the kitchen floor! Yes, I guarantee it. No matter which opinion you settle on, the fact remains, my friend once told me that I could put the whole darn squash in the slow cooker and walk away. Yes, I settled on *both* opinions she was crazy *and* clever all at the same time. Enjoy the ease of this recipe and let me know what your thoughts are!

Age and Stage: 6 months+ | Stage One | First Foods and Beyond
Slow Cooker Size: 4 to 6 quarts (3.8 to 5.7 l); oval

1 large butternut squash

1. Wash the squash and place the whole squash into the slow cooker. (This is not a joke!) If you'd like, lightly swipe olive oil on the bottom of the vessel to help prevent sticking; this is optional and I have never found the squash to stick. You could also add ½ cup water to the slow cooker, if desired, instead of the oil.
2. Cover and cook on high for 4 to 5 hours or on low for 6 to 8 hours. The squash will be cooked when it is easily pierced with a fork and the skin puckers a bit or gets wrinkly.
3. Remove the cooked squash from the slow cooker and allow to cool. Once cooled, cut the squash in half and remove the seeds. Scoop the flesh out of the shell and into a bowl.

Preparation and Storage for Baby

Place the squash in a blender or food processor and process to a texture that is appropriate for your baby. Add water, formula, or breast milk as desired to create a thin puree.

Store in the refrigerator for up to 3 days for babies.

To freeze, follow the stage one directions for beginner eaters in "Freezing Homemade Baby Food" on page 28.

For the Family

If you'd like to get a bit adventurous, make a curried squash soup with the puree by adding broth to thin to your desired consistency and 1 teaspoon of curry powder for starters. Stir and taste, then season as needed to achieve a perfect-for-you curry soup. Don't forget the dollop of yogurt or sour cream to finish.

❄ ?
🍎 ?
★ ?

Carrots for Everyone

A cold, peeled carrot—not chopped but left in all its orange glory—makes a very good teether. My boys would chomp and gum on carrots all day long when they were teething. Be sure to use long, fat carrots and trim off the thin end until you have a carrot that is uniformly thick and cannot be broken off.

Age and Stage: 6 months+ | Stage One | First Foods and Beyond
Slow Cooker Size: 4 to 6 quarts (3.8 to 5.7 l); deep or oval

3 pounds (1.4 kg) fresh carrots or 3 bags (1 pound [455 g] each) baby carrots
1 to 2 cups (235 to 475 ml) cold water
Pinch of ginger (optional)
Pinch of ground cinnamon (optional)
Drizzle of maple syrup (optional)

1. Wash and peel the carrots. Cut into large dice. Transfer the diced carrots to the slow cooker and cover with 1 cup water.
2. For babies over 8 months old, add the ginger, cinnamon, and maple syrup.
3. Cover and cook on low for 6 hours or on high for 4 hours. Check after about 4 hours (for low cooking) or 3 hours (for high cooking) and add the remaining 1 cup water if needed. Continue to cook until tender. Note that carrots won't cook down to a very smooth texture, so you'll probably need to puree them for a beginning eater.

Preparation and Storage for Baby

If the texture is appropriate for your baby straight from the slow cooker, set aside a portion or two for baby's meal and feed after the carrots have cooled. You could use a fork or spoon to mash the carrots in a small bowl. Otherwise, place the carrots in a blender or food processor and process to a texture that is appropriate for your baby. Add water, formula, or breast milk as desired to create a thin puree. Cooked carrots may also be frozen in diced form.

Store in the refrigerator for up to 3 days for babies.

To freeze, follow the stage one directions for beginner eaters in "Freezing Homemade Baby Food" on page 28.

For the Family

Serve the carrots as a side dish and freeze the remaining portion in freezer-safe containers. As with the winter squash (see page 60), you can also make a very yummy soup from the cooked carrots; try adding curry as your seasoning!

❄ Freezes well. 🍎 Vitamins A, C, and E, plus iron, potassium, calcium, and magnesium

Cauliflower: The Edible White Tree

Like broccoli, cauliflower makes a great puree and also a great finger food. Cauliflower was never a favorite food of my kids unless it was drenched in homemade cheese sauce. Not even grated cheese could tempt my little ones into eating cauliflower.

Age and Stage: 7 to 8 months+ | Stage One | First Foods and Beyond
Slow Cooker Size: 4 to 6 quarts (3.8 to 5.7 l); oval

3 pounds (1.4 kg) fresh cauliflower (about 3 heads)
¾ cup (175 ml) water

1. Remove the leaves from the cauliflower, if needed. Wash the cauliflower and then cut the florets from the stem. Discard the stem.
2. Transfer the florets to the slow cooker and add the water.
3. Cover and cook on low for 2 to 3 hours. You may want to remove some of the cauliflower sooner if you prefer al dente cauliflower for yourself and the older family members. Cauliflower florets will cook and soften to mush, though not as quickly as their broccoli brethren. You will need to puree the cauliflower if your baby is not eating textured foods yet. If she is enjoying texture and finger foods, lightly mash the florets and serve.

Preparation and Storage for Baby

If the texture of the cooked cauliflower is appropriate for finger food for your baby straight from the slow cooker, set aside a portion or two for baby's meal. Otherwise, place the cauliflower in a blender or food processor and process to a texture that is appropriate for your baby. Add water, formula, or breast milk as desired to create a thin puree.

Store in the refrigerator for up to 3 days for babies.

To freeze, follow the stage one directions for beginner eaters in "Freezing Homemade Baby Food" on page 28.

For the Family

Cauliflower is not very appealing for us big kids, so don't forget to remove some from the slow cooker prior to the mush stage. You can then roast the cauliflower in a 400°F (200°C) oven with a bit of olive oil and herbs and garlic.

> **Caution:** *Cauliflower can cause tummy upset as well as gas. It's better to wait until your baby is around 7 to 8 months of age before serving him cauliflower.*

❄ Freezes well, if pureed, but does not freeze well as is.
🍎 B vitamins, including folate, and A, a lot of C, and K, as well as fiber, calcium, and iron

Corn

Corn is great to use for finger exercising. The little niblets will keep your baby's fingers pinching away for hours. Remember that there are opportunities everywhere for your baby to develop fine-motor skills.

Age and Stage: 6 months+ | Stage One | First Foods and Beyond
Slow Cooker Size: 4 to 6 quarts (3.8 to 5.7 l); oval

6 ears corn
¾ cup (175 ml) water
Butter (optional)

1. Shuck the corn (remove the leaves and corn silk) and cut the ears in half, widthwise. Wash the ears and place in the slow cooker. Add the water.
2. If your baby doesn't have any dairy issues, add a few pats of butter. (Remember, some fats are good for baby!)
3. Cover and cook on high for 2 to 3 hours or until tender. Remove the cooked corn from the slow cooker and shave the kernels off the cobs. No matter how long you cook it, corn will not turn to mush. You will have to puree it to serve to your baby if she is still on thinner puree textures. If your baby is enjoying texture and finger foods, ensure that the corn kernels can be easily squished between the gums. Test by lightly squeezing a few kernels between your thumb and forefinger.

Preparation and Storage for Baby

If the texture is appropriate for your baby straight from the slow cooker, set aside a portion or two for baby's meal. Otherwise, place the corn kernels in a blender or food processor and process to a texture that is appropriate for your baby. You will need to add water, formula, or breast milk to create a thin puree.

Store in the refrigerator for up to 3 days for babies.

To freeze, follow the stage one directions for beginner eaters in "Freezing Homemade Baby Food" on page 28.

For the Family

Eat the corn off the cob or use the kernels that you shaved off to make creamed corn, to add to chowders and soups, or as a great addition to corn bread.

❄ Freezes well, if pureed, but you may see ice crystals build up on the puree. The kernels freeze well as is.
🍎 B vitamins, including folate, and A, plus protein, fiber, and iron   ★ Corn is considered to be allergenic; however, it is not one of the top eight most highly allergenic foods, and a corn allergy is not very common. Always consult with your pediatrician about food allergies and feeding baby solid foods. Keep in mind that corn is not easily digested and is not suitable as a first food.

Green Beans: It's Not Easy Being Green

Stringy and a bit tough but easy to pick up, green beans are good for tossing to the dog from the high chair. My kids preferred green beans chopped and a bit al dente but really loved them when pureed with applesauce, too. If there's one thing for certain when it comes to feeding babies, what they like will constantly change, so keep offering the "hated" food of the day and, eventually, you may find your baby loves it!

Age and Stage: 6 months+ | Stage One | First Foods and Beyond
Slow Cooker Size: 4 to 6 quarts (3.8 to 5.7 l); oval

3 pounds (1.4 kg) fresh green beans
2 cups (475 ml) water or no-salt chicken broth

1. Wash the green beans and snap or trim off the ends.
2. Place the green beans in the slow cooker and add the water or broth.
3. Cover and cook on high for 2 to 3 hours or until tender. Check them often; green beans will turn to mush if you cook them long enough. If your baby is enjoying texture and finger foods, keep an eye on them so they don't overcook. Remove the green beans from the slow cooker and set aside to cool.

Preparation and Storage for Baby

Place the cooled green beans (which will puree more smoothly than hot beans) in a blender or food processor and process to a texture that is appropriate for your baby. Add water, formula, or breast milk as needed to create a thin puree for your beginning eater.

Store in the refrigerator for up to 3 days for babies.

To freeze, follow the stage one directions for beginner eaters in "Freezing Homemade Baby Food" on page 28.

For the Family

Of course, you must make a green bean casserole with any extra green beans!

❄ Freezes well, if pureed, but you may see ice crystals build up on the puree.
🍍 B vitamins, including folate, and A, C, and K as well as fiber, calcium, iron, and manganese

Lentils: A Fablous Source of Nutrition!

"When-tills," as my kids used to call them, are super versatile and contain an amazing array of nutrients. You can make them al dente or mushy and puree them into anything you want. As a finger food, lentils only increase frustration due to their small size and slippery nature. Let baby dig through a whole bowl of cooked lentils rather than plopping a few on the tray.

Age and Stage: 6 months+ | Stage One | First Foods and Beyond
Slow Cooker Size: 4 to 6 quarts (3.8 to 5.7 l); oval

3 cups (576 g) dried lentils
1 carrot (optional)
2 cups (475 ml) water

1. Rinse and pick through the lentils to ensure that no debris winds up in the slow cooker. If your baby has had carrots, wash, peel, and chop the carrot.
2. Transfer the lentils and carrot (if using) to the slow cooker. Add the water and stir to combine.
3. Cover and cook on low for 5 to 7 hours, or until tender, stirring occasionally. Lentils will melt and turn to mush if you cook them long enough. You may not even have to puree them. Remove the lentils from the slow cooker and set aside to cool.

Preparation and Storage for Baby

If needed, place the lentils in a blender or food processor and process to a texture that is appropriate for your baby. Add water, formula, or breast milk as needed to create a thin puree for your beginning eater.

Store in the refrigerator for up to 3 days for babies.

To freeze, follow the stage one directions for beginner eaters in "Freezing Homemade Baby Food" on page 28.

For the Family

Lentils can be turned into soup or make a great side dish. You can also make hummus with lentils and spice them up with curry spices. We like to add diced chicken, onion, black beans, and carrots to make a quick lentil stew. Cook up extra portions and make stew or freeze them for later.

❄ Freezes well, if pureed, but you may see ice crystals build up on the puree and some separation may occur.
● B vitamins and K as well as fiber, iron, and calcium. One cup of lentils has 90 percent of the daily requirement of folate!

Parsnips: Hooray for Roots!

Parsnips are another great finger food for little ones, but they also make a fantastic puree. If you mix them with beets, you'll end up with a wonderful pink hue that really catches the eyes of babies!

Age and Stage: 6 months+ | Stage One | First Foods and Beyond
Slow Cooker Size: 4 to 6 quarts (3.8 to 5.7 l); oval

3 pounds (1.4 kg) parsnips
2 cups (475 ml) water

1. Wash, peel, and roughly chop the parsnips.
2. Transfer the parsnips to the slow cooker. Add the water.
3. Cover and cook on low for 5 to 7 hours or on high for 3 to 4 hours or until tender. (Parsnips may need longer in the slow cooker than other veggies. These lovely roots have a woody center that does not soften easily.) Once soft, remove the parsnips from the slow cooker and set aside to cool.

Preparation and Storage for Baby

Place the parsnips in a blender or food processor and process to a texture that is appropriate for your baby. Add water, formula, or breast milk as needed to create a thin puree for your beginning eater.

Store in the refrigerator for up to 3 days for babies.

To freeze, follow the stage one directions for beginner eaters in "Freezing Homemade Baby Food" on page 28.

For the Family

If you haven't slow-cooked the parsnips down to a mushy texture, place some of the parsnips on a baking sheet, drizzle them with olive oil, and season with dried oregano, rosemary, and thyme. Then pop under a broiler for 10 to 15 minutes. Enjoy! And be sure to check out the Root Veggie Trio on page 111.

❄ Freezes well if pureed, also freezes nicely in "sticks."
🍎 B vitamins, including folate, and C and E, as well as fiber, iron, and calcium

Peas—Yes!

As my twins grew older, they found that they could play handball with peas. It didn't matter if I put the peas in bowls; they would pick them out and bat them back and forth across their high chair trays. Now playing with food is important, but after so many peas fly through the air, you must put a stop to it.

Age and Stage: 6 months+ | Stage One | First Foods and Beyond
Slow Cooker Size: 4 to 6 quarts (3.8 to 5.7 l); oval

> 3 bags (1 pound [455 g] each) frozen green peas
> 1 cup (235 ml) water

1. Pour the peas into the slow cooker. Add the water.
2. Cover and cook on low for 5 to 7 hours or on high for 3 to 4 hours or until tender. Peas don't cook down to a soft texture very easily, so check often and add more water if needed. When they're tender, remove the peas from the slow cooker and set aside to cool. Then place in the refrigerator. Peas will make a smoother puree if they're cold.

Preparation and Storage for Baby

Place the peas in a blender or food processor and process to a texture that is appropriate for your baby. Add water, formula, or breast milk as needed to create a thin puree for your beginning eater.

Adding a bit of mint to pea puree creates a lovely flavor for babies and adults, alike.

Store in the refrigerator for up to 3 days for babies.

To freeze, follow the stage one directions for beginner eaters in "Freezing Homemade Baby Food" on page 28.

For the Family

Peas can be the star of the side dish or can be tossed into almost any dish imaginable. One of my favorite things to do with peas is to put them in homemade mac and cheese, make macaroni salad with chicken and peas, mix them with carrots (of course!), or lightly drizzle them with lemon balsamic and rosemary olive oil and just eat them cold as a snack.

❄ Freezes well, if pureed.   ● B vitamins, including folate, and A, C, and K, as well as fiber, iron, and calcium!

Pumpkins

Whenever you cook pumpkin, or any winter squash for that matter, don't throw out the seeds. Save them and roast them. The seeds of winter squash are incredibly nutritious, but sadly, not for children under the age of 8. Well, 8 is the age that I first felt comfortable letting my kids eat the seeds.

Age and Stage: 6 months+ | Stage One | First Foods and Beyond
Slow Cooker Size: 6 quarts (5.7 l); oval

> 2 sugar pumpkins (2 to 4 pounds [907 g to 1.8 kg] each)
> 1 to 2 cups (235 to 475 ml) water

METHOD 1
1. Wash the pumpkins and cut off the stems. Cut in half and remove the seeds. Peel the pumpkins.
2. Roughly chop the pumpkin flesh and place in the slow cooker. Add 1 cup water.
3. Cover and cook on low for 5 to 7 hours or on high for 2 to 3 hours, or until tender. Mash the pumpkin in the slow cooker. Remove the pumpkin and set aside to cool.

METHOD 2
1. Wash the pumpkins and cut off the stems. Cut in half and remove the seeds.
2. Place the pumpkin halves in the slow cooker skin side up. Add 2 cups water, or enough to cover the bottom of the slow cooker.
3. Cover and cook on low for 5 to 7 hours or on high for 2 to 3 hours or until tender. Remove the pumpkin halves from the slow cooker and set aside to cool. Once cooled, scrape out the pumpkin flesh and then mash or puree as needed.

Preparation and Storage for Baby

Pumpkin cooks down nicely in the slow cooker, so you may not have to puree it for your baby. If you do, place the pumpkin in a blender or food processor and process to a texture that is appropriate for your baby. Add water, formula, or breast milk as needed to create a thin puree for your beginning eater.

Store in the refrigerator for up to 3 days for babies.

To freeze, follow the stage one directions for beginner eaters in "Freezing Homemade Baby Food" on page 28.

For the Family

Pumpkin is such a versatile squash. You can mix in some cinnamon and nutmeg or add savory herbs and spices such as thyme, rosemary, sage, and pepper and serve as a side dish.

Sugar pumpkins are also called baking pumpkins. On average, they weigh 2 to 4 pounds (907 g. to 1.8 kg.) and are much smaller than jack-o'-lantern pumpkins. Sugar pumpkins tend to be less fibrous and stringy and make a really great puree for a variety of dishes and recipes.

❋ Freezes well, if pureed, but may separate.   🍎 B vitamins, including folate, and A (245 percent of the daily requirement in a 1-cup serving!) and C as well as fiber, iron, and calcium

Spaghetti Squash

Spaghetti squash is one of the funnest foods to play with, and my family loves that you can eat it like it's a veggie or like it's pasta. When your kids are toddlers, let them play with this stringy veggie and enjoy the feel of it as it slips through their fingers. I recommend skipping the red pasta sauce for food play with spaghetti squash!

Age and Stage: 6 months+ | Stage One | First Foods and Beyond
Slow Cooker Size: 6 quarts (5.7 l); oval

1 spaghetti squash (4 to 6 pounds [1.8 to 2.7 kg]; make sure that the squash is not overly large so that you can still fit the lid on your slow cooker)
½ cup (120 ml) water

1. Wash the squash and cut in half. Remove the stem.
2. Place the squash halves in the slow cooker skin side up. Add the water.
3. Cover and cook on low for 5 to 7 hours or on high for 2 to 3 hours or until tender. Remove from the slow cooker and allow to cool. When cool to the touch, run a fork lengthwise down the spaghetti squash, scraping out the flesh. The squash will come apart in spaghetti-like strings.

Preparation and Storage for Baby

Spaghetti squash will cook down nicely in the slow cooker, but due to its stringiness, you will have to puree it for beginners. Place the spaghetti squash flesh in a blender or food processor and process to a texture that is appropriate for your baby. Add water, formula, or breast milk as needed to create a thin puree for your beginning eater.

Store in the refrigerator for up to 3 days for babies.

To freeze, follow the stage one directions for beginner eaters in "Freezing Homemade Baby Food" on page 28.

For the Family

I love to toss cooked spaghetti squash with olive oil and garlic and then lightly sauté. Another way to serve this squash is by tossing it with marinara sauce and sprinkling with grated cheese. You could also make Alfredo carbonara and toss it with Alfredo sauce and mix in some peas.

❄ Does not really freeze well, whole, but will freeze if pureed.
🍎 Vitamins A, B, and C, and some iron and calcium

Sweet Potatoes: A Yam Good Veggie

As a first food, you can't beat the sweet potato. When I fed my kids pureed sweet potatoes, they would try to grab the spoon from me and become impatient if I didn't feed them fast enough. When they moved into toddlerhood, diced cubes of sweet potatoes were never rejected.

Age and Stage: 6 months+ | Stage One | First Foods and Beyond
Slow Cooker Size: 6 quarts (5.7 l); oval

8 medium to large sweet potatoes
½ cup (120 ml) water
2 pats butter

1. Wash the sweet potatoes and peel them. Roughly chop and transfer to the slow cooker.
2. Add the water. Cover and cook on low for 5 to 7 hours or on high for 3 to 4 hours or until tender. Mash the butter into the sweet potatoes in the slow cooker and then remove and set aside to cool.

Preparation and Storage for Baby

If necessary, place the sweet potatoes in a blender or food processor and process to a texture that is appropriate for your baby. Add water, formula, or breast milk as needed to create a thin puree for your beginning eater.

Store in the refrigerator for up to 3 days for babies.

To freeze, follow the stage one directions for beginner eaters in "Freezing Homemade Baby Food" on page 28.

For the Family

Sweet potatoes make a wonderful side dish and can be served sweet (with cinnamon and brown sugar) or savory (with butter and rosemary, thyme, and sage). Add these flavors to the cooked sweet potatoes and warm to infuse.

❄ Freezes well, if pureed   🍎 1 cup of sweet potatoes contains 1,053 percent of the daily value of vitamin A! Vitamin A is a carotenoid. Some babies who eat a lot of vegetables that are high in vitamin A will develop an orange tinge on their cheeks, the soles of their feet, and the palms of their hands. Don't worry, though, this is not a health hazard and will subside once the levels decrease. Sweet potatoes also contain vitamins B, C, E, and K as well as some iron, calcium, and manganese.

Summer Squash

Zucchini, pattypan, and yellow squash were guaranteed to bring a frowny face to my twins, unless the squash was mixed with applesauce or pears. I know, now you are making a frowny face. Sometimes, you just have to get creative when serving new and old tastes and textures.

Age and Stage: 6 months+ | Stage One | First Foods and Beyond
Slow Cooker Size: 6 quarts (5.7 l); oval

4 zucchini
4 yellow/crookneck squash
2 tablespoons (28 ml) water
2 teaspoons olive oil

1. Wash the zucchini and yellow squash. Slice into uniform "coins."
2. Transfer the coins to the slow cooker. Add the water and olive oil.
3. Cover and cook on low for 2 hours or until tender. If needed, mash the squash in the slow cooker and then remove and set aside to cool.

Preparation and Storage for Baby

If needed, place the squash in a blender or food processor and process to a texture that is appropriate for your baby. Add water, formula, or breast milk as needed to create a thin puree for your beginning eater.

Store in the refrigerator for up to 3 days for babies.

To freeze, follow the stage one directions for beginner eaters in "Freezing Homemade Baby Food" on page 28.

For the Family

I have to say, the best way to prepare summer squash, especially zucchini, is to stuff it with rice and other veggies and then bake it. What will you do with all this slow cooker summer squash? You should make bread, of course!

❄ Freezes well, if pureed, but may become watery when thawed.
● Vitamins A, B, C, E, and K as well as calcium and a little bit of iron

Turnips: Who Would Have Thought?

Turnips are a bit bitter and may not be a favorite of babies when pureed. This is one of the veggies that you may want to try as finger food cubes instead of puree. Remember to keep those tiny fingers pinching so your baby can continue to develop fine-motor skills!

Age and Stage: 6 months+ | Stage One | First Foods and Beyond
Slow Cooker Size: 6 quarts (5.7 l); oval

4 purple turnips
1 cup (235 ml) water

1. Wash and peel the turnips. Roughly chop into cubes.
2. Transfer the turnip cubes to the slow cooker. Add the water.
3. Cover and cook on low for 5 to 7 hours or on high for 3 to 4 hours, or until tender. Mash the turnips in the slow cooker and then remove and set aside to cool.

Preparation and Storage for Baby

Place the turnips in a blender or food processor and process to a texture that is appropriate for your baby. Add water, formula, or breast milk as needed to create a thin puree for your beginning eater.

Store in the refrigerator for up to 3 days for babies.

To freeze, follow the stage one directions for beginner eaters in "Freezing Homemade Baby Food" on page 28.

For the Family

Before the turnips turn to complete baby mush, take some out of the slow cooker and set them aside for your side dish. I like to add sage and butter and mash them into the turnips. If the turnips are al dente, you can drizzle them with olive oil and sprinkle with Italian seasoning and roast until tender.

> *Keep in mind that turnips may cause painful gas for some babies.*
>

❄ Freezes well, if pureed, but may become watery when thawed.
🍎 Vitamins B, C, E, and K as well as calcium and a little bit of iron

White Potatoes

White potatoes are a lot of fun for babies: You just plop a scoop down on the high chair tray and let baby dig in. This is a great food to practice spoon skills with because the potatoes will stick to the spoon and decrease frustration! Plop down some pureed beets along with white potatoes and show baby how to mix them together. The color pink will quickly appear. Science at the dining table!

Age and Stage: 6 months+ | Stage One | First Foods and Beyond
Slow Cooker Size: 6 quarts (5.7 l); oval

5 pounds (2.3 kg) russet potatoes
1 cup (235 ml) water

1. Wash and peel the potatoes. Cut into chunks.
2. Transfer the potatoes to the slow cooker. Add the water.
3. Cover and cook on low for 5 to 7 hours or on high for 3 to 4 hours or until tender. Mash the potatoes in the slow cooker and then remove and set aside to cool.

Preparation and Storage for Baby

Even after mashing the potatoes, you may still need to puree them for beginner eaters. If so, place the potatoes in a blender or food processor and process to a texture that is appropriate for your baby. Add water, formula, or breast milk as needed to create a thin puree for your beginning eater. Be careful: if you overprocess the potatoes, you may end up with a gluey, gloopy, wallpaper-pastey mess that no one wants to eat.

Store the potato puree in the refrigerator for up to 3 days for babies.

To freeze, follow the stage one directions for beginner eaters in "Freezing Homemade Baby Food" on page 28.

For the Family

Before the potatoes turn to complete baby mush, take some out of the slow cooker and set them aside for your side dish. I like to add minced garlic and butter and mash them into the potatoes. You could also make potato balls.

❄ Freezes well, but may become separated and watery when thawed.
● Vitamins B and C as well as a little bit of iron, plus calcium and protein

Cooking Meat in the Slow Cooker

It was once the rule that you should never place raw meat into a slow cooker and that meat should always be seared and pan cooked prior to going into the slow cooker. Food safety experts now agree that as long as the meat is cooked to its proper temperature, it is safe to use raw meats in the slow cooker. The following are the appropriate temperatures for cooked meat:

- Beef: 160°F (70°C)
- Poultry: 165°F (75°C)
- Pork: 160°F (70°C)
- Fish: 145°F (65°C)

Most slow cookers will cook between 190°F and 300°F (90°C and 150°C).

Use a meat thermometer to ensure that all meat you serve to your baby is at the safe temperature.

The best cuts of meat to cook in a slow cooker are those that have more fat and are not as lean. For poultry, the dark meat will cook up more tender than the light. Here are a few examples of meats that do really well in the slow cooker, cooking up moist and tender and juicy.

- Beef chuck roast
- Beef brisket
- Beef "pot" roast
- Pork butt
- Pork shoulder
- Chicken thighs
- Chicken drumsticks
- Lamb shank

Beef

Beef puree will be one of the most difficult things to feed to your baby. It's not appealing at all to adults, but do remember that your baby really has no idea what is appealing or unappealing!

Age and Stage: 6 months+ | Stage One | First Foods and Beyond
Slow Cooker Size: 6 quarts (5.7 l); oval

2 pounds (907 g) chuck roast
1 cup (235 ml) water

1. If desired, sear the roast in a hot skillet with olive oil prior to placing in the slow cooker. If you do so, be sure to deglaze the skillet and put the juices into the slow cooker.
2. Put the seared or raw roast in the slow cooker. Add the water.
3. Cover and cook on low for 7 to 8 hours or on high for 4 to 5 hours or until a thermometer inserted in the center of the roast registers 160°F (70°C) and there is no pink remaining. Remove the roast from the slow cooker and set it aside to cool for at least 5 minutes. You may shred or cut the roast while it is still warm.

Preparation and Storage for Baby

Puree the beef when it is cold. Cold meats puree better than warm or hot meats do. Though you can use a blender to do this, a food processor will make a smoother beef puree. Process the meat to a texture that is appropriate for your baby. Add water, formula, or breast milk as needed to create a thin puree for your beginning eater.

Store the puree in the refrigerator for up to 3 days for babies.

To freeze, follow the stage one directions for beginner eaters in "Freezing Homemade Baby Food" on page 28.

For the Family

You could serve the roast, as is, with side dishes or shred some of it and season with taco seasonings to make beef tacos. Or you could even make barbecue beef by simmering the meat in barbecue sauce.

> *Remember, it is not necessary to sear meat prior to cooking it in a slow cooker. There are occasions where I will sear meat for color or to lock in juices (if I have the time and inclination), and many when I do not. It is up to you whether to sear or not.*

※ Freezes well, but may become separated, gritty, and watery when thawed. When you warm it up, vigorously mix to recombine.   🍎 B vitamins, iron, and protein

Super Easy Chicken

While this chicken recipe is super easy, getting your kids to eat chicken puree might not be as easy. Because meat and poultry purees may be a bit grainy, your baby may reject them at first. Keep offering but don't force, and if you want, mix in some peaches or butternut squash!

Age and Stage: 6 months+ | Stage One | First Foods and Beyond
Slow Cooker Size: 4 to 6 quarts (3.8 to 5.7 l); oval

> 1 whole chicken (5 to 6 pounds)
> 1 cup (235 ml) cold water
> ½ lemon
> 1 tablespoon (15 ml) olive oil

1. Wash the chicken in the sink on a cutting board. Place the chicken in the slow cooker and add the water.
2. Squeeze the lemon half over the chicken and drizzle with the olive oil.
3. Cover and cook on low for 6 hours or on high for 4 hours or until a thermometer inserted in a breast registers at least 165°F (75°C).

Preparation and Storage for Baby

Chicken and other meats puree best when they have cooled for a while; just think about how much easier it is to slice chicken when it has been cooled. It's the same with pureeing.

To puree chicken, use a food processor to reduce the chicken to a crumbly, powderlike texture and then add water, formula, or breast milk as needed as you continue to puree.

Store in the refrigerator for up to 3 days for babies.

To freeze, follow the stage one directions for beginner eaters in "Freezing Homemade Baby Food" on page 28.

For the Family

Serve the chicken as the entrée. Make chicken salad for lunches. Shred it and make chicken soup, or dice it and make a chicken potpie. The ways to use a slow-cooked chicken are really limited only by your imagination.

❄ Freezes well, but may become separated, gritty, and watery when thawed. When you warm it up, vigorously stir to reconstitute. 🍎 Vitamins B_6 and B_{12}, iron, potassium, calcium, magnesium, and protein

Haddock: Fish Ahoy!

Haddock is easily pureed and becomes nice and creamy. It's a great fish to puree, but it's an even better finger food. When haddock is baked, broiled, poached, or even lightly fried, it will flake beautifully. My kids preferred fish that was served up as finger food, especially when smothered in pear sauce!

Age and Stage: 6 months+ | Stage One | First Foods and Beyond

Slow Cooker Size: 4 to 6 quarts (3.8 to 5.7 l); oval

3 pounds (1.4 kg) haddock fillets
¼ cup (60 ml) cold water

1. Lightly rinse the haddock and remove any wayward bones. Pat the fillets dry with a paper towel.
2. Place the fillets in the slow cooker. Add the water.
3. Cover and cook on low for 6 hours or on high for 2 to 3 hours or until the haddock turns white and flakes easily. Remove the fish from the slow cooker and transfer to a cutting board to cool.

Preparation and Storage for Baby

Fish will puree easily whether it's hot or cold. To puree the haddock, use a food processor to reduce it to a crumbly, powderlike texture and then add water, formula, or breast milk as needed as you continue to puree.

For finger food, use a fork to just gently separate the fish so that it flakes.

Store in the refrigerator for up to 3 days for babies.

To freeze, follow the stage one directions for beginner eaters in "Freezing Homemade Baby Food" on page 28. You can also freeze chunks of the cooked haddock and use as needed. Haddock flakes make great finger food for babies learning how to self-feed.

For the Family

Serve haddock as the entrée. Drizzle it with olive oil and sprinkle with minced garlic and some pepper and then heat under the broiler for 6 minutes. Or why not use some of the haddock to create a fish chowder?

❄ Freezes well, but the puree may become separated, gritty, and watery when thawed. When you warm it up, vigorously mix to recombine. It's best to freeze the haddock fillets whole or in flakes. 🍎 One haddock fillet contains 73 percent of the daily value of protein! It's high in B vitamins, iron, potassium, calcium, and magnesium, too!

Lamb: Do We Have To?

I have never ever liked lamb, not even when it was smothered in layers of mint jelly. However, because we as parents have the responsibility of not transferring our food aversion to our children, I did make lamb for my kids. Once. Only once. Thankfully, they inherited my taste buds!

Age and Stage: 6 months+ | Stage One | First Foods and Beyond
Slow Cooker Size: 4 to 6 quarts (3.8 to 5.7 l); oval

2 tablespoons (28 ml) olive oil
4 lamb shanks or lamb chops
½ cup (120 ml) water

1. In a skillet, heat the oil over medium-high heat. Pat the lamb dry with a paper towel. Place in the skillet and brown on all sides.
2. Transfer the lamb to the slow cooker. Deglaze the skillet and add the juices to the slow cooker. Add the water.
3. Cover and cook on low for 6 to 7 hours or until a thermometer inserted in the center of a shank or chop registers 160°F (70°C) and no pink remains.

Preparation and Storage for Baby

For finger food, dice the lamb into small but manageable cubes. Lamb will puree easily when it's cold.

To puree the lamb, use a food processor to reduce it to a crumbly, powderlike texture and then add water, formula, or breast milk as needed as you continue to puree.

Store in the refrigerator for up to 3 days for babies.

To freeze, follow the stage one directions for beginner eaters in "Freezing Homemade Baby Food" on page 28. You can also freeze chunks of the cooked lamb and use them as needed. Diced lamb makes a great finger food for babies learning how to self-feed.

For the Family

I don't serve lamb, and no one in my immediate family eats it. My grandmother would serve it with mint jelly and roasted carrots and mashed potatoes. Fond memories of Gramma, indeed.

❈ Freezes well, but the puree may become separated, gritty, and watery when thawed. When you warm it up, vigorously mix to recombine.   🍎 Vitamins B_6 and B_{12}, iron, potassium, calcium, and magnesium, plus a lot of protein

Pork

Pork is great to give babies as a first meat. It's a very mild-tasting and smooth-textured meat. Try mixing the puree with applesauce or drizzle some applesauce over diced pork.

Age and Stage: 6 months+ | Stage One | First Foods and Beyond
Slow Cooker Size: 4 to 6 quarts (3.8 to 5.7 l); oval

> 2 tablespoons (28 ml) olive oil
> 1 pork butt roast (3 pounds [1.4 kg])

1. In a skillet, heat the oil over medium-high heat. Add the pork roast and brown on all sides.
2. Transfer the roast to the slow cooker. Deglaze the skillet and add the juices to the slow cooker.
3. Cover and cook on low for 6 to 7 hours or on high for 4 to 5 hours or until a thermometer inserted in the center registers 160°F (70°C) and no pink remains.

Preparation and Storage for Baby

For finger food, dice the pork into small but manageable cubes. Pork will puree easily when it's cold.

To puree the pork, use a food processor to reduce it to a crumbly, powderlike texture and then add water, formula, or breast milk as needed as you continue to puree.

Store in the refrigerator for up to 3 days for babies.

To freeze, follow the stage one directions for beginner eaters in "Freezing Homemade Baby Food" on page 28. You can also freeze chunks of the cooked pork and use them as needed. Diced pork makes a great finger food for babies learning how to self-feed.

For the Family

Whenever I make a pork roast in the slow cooker, I like to shred some for tacos and also for pulled pork. If you cook a loin roast in the slow cooker (in this recipe, we used the butt roast for more tender meat), you could use half for a meal for the family and half to puree and store for baby food.

❅ Freezes well, but the puree may become separated, gritty, and watery when thawed. When you warm it up, vigorously mix to recombine. 🍎 High in B vitamins, iron, potassium, calcium, and magnesium, and a lot of protein

Salmon

Salmon is another great first protein to offer babies. When you give cooked salmon flakes to your baby, you'll encourage a love of healthy fish and also help those fine-motor skills! One day, you may even hear your toddler ask for "the orange fish, I want dat."

Age and Stage: 6 months+ | Stage One | First Foods and Beyond
Slow Cooker Size: 4 to 6 quarts (3.8 to 5.7 l); oval

1 large salmon fillet (2 to 3 pounds [907 g to 1.4 kg]), skin removed
2 tablespoons (28 ml) olive oil

1. Carefully inspect the salmon fillet and discard any bones. Cut the fillet into thirds.
2. Transfer the salmon to the slow cooker. Drizzle with the olive oil.
3. Cover and cook on low for 6 to 7 hours or until the salmon is opaque and flakes easily with a fork.

Preparation and Storage for Baby

For finger food, flake the salmon into manageable pieces.

Salmon will puree easily whether it's hot or cold. To puree the salmon, use a blender or a food processor and add water, formula, or breast milk as needed as you puree.

Store in the refrigerator for up to 3 days for babies.

To freeze, follow the stage one directions for beginner eaters in "Freezing Homemade Baby Food" on page 28. You can also freeze pieces of the cooked salmon and use them as needed. Flaked or diced salmon makes a great finger food for babies learning how to self-feed.

For the Family

Serve some of the salmon as the entrée. Drizzle with olive oil, sprinkle with minced garlic, dill, and some pepper, and then broil for 6 minutes.

❄ Freezes well, but the puree may become separated, gritty, and watery when thawed. When you warm it up, vigorously mix to recombine. It's best to freeze the salmon in pieces or flakes. ● Salmon is loaded with B vitamins, though it is best known for its omega-3 content. Omega-3 fats are "good fats" and help with brain development, eye health, muscular and connective tissue health, and so much more. Including salmon in your diet is incredibly beneficial to overall health.

Second Foods:
Fruit and Vegetable Combinations

The delicious fruit and veggie combinations in this chapter are designated as Stage Two, for those babies who are 8 months and older. These recipes are also appropriate for those Stage One tiny foodies who already have many foods, and even some herbs and spices, in their food repertoire.

Earlier in this book we discussed the 3- to 4-day wait rule that reminds us to introduce one new food at a time and then wait for 3 to 4 days to see if your baby has a reaction to that food. If you're introducing any new foods in Stage Two, you'll once again want to follow this rule. Once baby has tried a variety of foods, you can then begin to mix a few ingredients together and make combination meals. If your younger baby has had each food individually and has done well, feel free to serve him these combinations that are cooked together.

Now the fun and taste exploration can truly begin! If you haven't already been adding extra flavor to your baby's food with herbs and spices, try doing so now! See the list on page 40 for some great ideas. (Keep in mind that besides the flavor boost, these herbs and spices have health benefits, too.) And if you have been using them, explore new varieties to please your baby's palate. Beyond that, this is also the stage to start creating interesting food combinations and scrumptious meals from a variety of foods.

The recipes that follow can be made as stand-alone "meals" for your baby but may also be used in a variety of other "meal" foods as well. The Pumpkin and Apples recipe on page 108, for example, can be a single meal or can be mixed into yogurt, oatmeal, another veggie or fruit, or a variety of meat purees and other foods.

Please note that none of the recipes in this chapter contain foods that are considered to be allergenic. However, you should always work with your pediatrician to ensure that foods are appropriate for your baby.

These recipes are also appropriate for those
Stage One tiny foodies who already have many foods,
and even some herbs and spices, in their food repertoire.

Apples and Carrots

The mix of apples and carrots is especially enticing for little ones when you serve this as finger food. Keep the carrots in chunks (mash or cut them into smaller bits if needed) and then spoon the applesauce over them. Yes, it will be messy, but it's so much fun!

Age and Stage: (6) 8 months+ | Stage Two | Second Foods and Beyond

Slow Cooker Size: 4 to 6 quarts (3.8 to 5.7 l); oval

1 pound (455 g) carrots
6 large apples, such as McIntosh
1 cup (235 ml) cold water
¼ teaspoon ground cinnamon (optional)

1. Wash the carrots and apples. Peel and roughly chop the carrots. Core, peel, and roughly chop the apples.
2. Place the carrots and apples into the slow cooker. Add the cinnamon, if using, and stir to combine.
3. Cover and cook on low for 5 to 6 hours or on high for 4 hours. You may need to add more water during the cooking process, so check after 3 hours. When done, the apples will be nicely simmered down while the carrots should remain soft but not overly mushy. Remove from the slow cooker and set aside to cool.

Preparation and Storage for Baby

When cooled, puree the food in batches. Use a food processor to achieve a smooth texture and add water, formula, or breast milk as you continue to puree. You can also partially puree the apples and carrots so that the food has some lumps to help baby make the transition to table foods.

Using a slotted spoon, remove some of the carrots and then spoon out some of the apples; set aside to offer as a finger food meal.

Store in the refrigerator for up to 3 days for babies.

To freeze, follow the stage two directions in "Freezing Homemade Baby Food" on page 28. You can also freeze the carrots and apples as they are and use as needed.

For the Family

Serve this mix as a delicious side dish. Prior to pureeing the mixture for your baby, remove some of the carrots and apples and set aside. Add these reserved portions to salads or reduce to make a soup.

❄ Freezes well, but some separation may occur when thawed, mix to recombine.
🍎 Vitamins A, B, C, E, and K, plus a little bit of iron and calcium

Apples and Sweet Potatoes

This dish is like Thanksgiving in a slow cooker, and your baby will thank you for making it. Whether you puree or mash up the apple and sweet potato mixture for self-feeding, this is a wonderful meal for babies.

Age and Stage: (6) 8 months+ | Stage Two | Second Foods and Beyond

Slow Cooker Size: 4 to 6 quarts (3.8 to 5.7 l); oval

   3 large sweet potatoes
   6 large apples, such as McIntosh
   1 cup (235 ml) cold water
   ¼ teaspoon ground cinnamon (optional)
   ¼ teaspoon ground nutmeg (optional)

1. Wash the sweet potatoes and apples. Peel and then chop the sweet potatoes into small but relatively uniform chunks. Halve, core, and peel the apples. Roughly chop them into chunks.
2. Transfer the sweet potatoes and apples to the slow cooker. Add the water. If using, add the cinnamon and nutmeg. Stir to combine.
3. Cover and cook on low for 5 to 6 hours or on high for 4 hours. After 3 hours of cooking time, check and add more water if needed. The apples will simmer down nicely, while the sweet potatoes should be soft but not overly mushy. It is possible that the sweet potatoes may need additional time to cook. If so, you can opt to remove the apples and continue to cook the sweet potatoes, or just set the timer, for 1 hour.

Preparation and Storage for Baby

Transfer the apples and sweet potatoes to a bowl to cool. Using a slotted spoon, remove some of the sweet potatoes and then spoon out some of the apples; set aside to offer as a finger food meal.
Puree the remaining food in batches. Use a food processor to achieve a smooth texture and add water, formula, or breast milk as you continue to puree. You can also partially puree the apples and sweet potatoes so that the food has some lumps to help baby make the transition to "table foods."

   Store in the refrigerator for up to 3 days for babies.

   To freeze, follow the stage two directions in "Freezing Homemade Baby Food" on page 28.

For the Family

Serve this mix as a delicious side dish. Prior to reducing the combo to a texture suitable for your baby, remove some of the sweet potatoes and apples and set aside. Or, when you have made enough baby food, keep the remaining sweet potatoes and apples in the slow cooker and reduce them to a butter; add some maple syrup, a bit of brown sugar, and cinnamon, vanilla, and nutmeg to taste.

❄ Freezes well, but some separation may occur when thawed; mix to recombine.
🍎 Vitamins A, B, C, E, and K and a little bit of iron and calcium

Apricots and Pears

For this combination, you will find that the pears help to offset the stickiness of the apricots. This is a tasty combination, but it doesn't make for a great finger food/self-feeding experience.

Age and Stage: (6) 8 months+ | Stage Two | Second Foods and Beyond
Slow Cooker Size: 4 to 6 quarts (3.8 to 5.7 l); oval

6 pears, such as red or Anjou
1½ pounds (683 g) dried apricots, unsulfured
1 teaspoon vanilla extract
1 cup (235 ml) cold water

1. Wash, halve, and core the pears. Then peel and roughly chop them.
2. Transfer the pears and apricots to the slow cooker. Add the vanilla and water. Stir to combine.
3. Cover and cook on low for 5 hours or on high for 2 hours. After 2 hours on low or 1 hour on high, check and add more water if needed. The pears will simmer down very soft, while the apricots may remain thick and sticky. When the apricots have been reduced to a thick, less sticky sauce, remove the fruits from the slow cooker and set aside to cool.

Preparation and Storage for Baby

When the fruits have cooled, puree the food in batches. Use a food processor to achieve a smooth texture and add water, formula, or breast milk as you continue to puree.

Store in the refrigerator for up to 3 days for babies.

To freeze, follow the stage two directions in "Freezing Homemade Baby Food" on page 28.

For the Family

Serve this mix as a delicious sauce or spread for toast, muffins, and biscuits or even over chicken or pork roast.

❄ Freezes well, but you may see ice crystals. Some separation may occur when thawed; mix to recombine
🍎 Vitamins A and C, fiber, and a little bit of iron and calcium

Apples and Beets with Ginger

Who wouldn't like to eat purple applesauce? Your older baby will absolutely love this combination and also enjoy watching her fingers turn red.

Age and Stage: (6) 8 months+ | Stage Two | Second Foods and Beyond
Slow Cooker Size: 4 to 6 quarts (3.8 to 5.7 l); oval

4 large apples, such as McIntosh
4 large beets
½ cup (120 ml) cold water
¼ teaspoon pureed or grated fresh ginger

1. Wash the apples and beets. Halve, core, and peel the apples, then roughly chop them. Peel the beets and chop them into small but relatively uniform chunks.
2. Transfer the apples and beets to the slow cooker. Add the water and ginger. Stir to combine.
3. Cover and cook on low for 4 hours, checking after 3 hours and adding more water if needed. After 4 hours, check the texture of the beets. If they are soft-cooked, remove the beets and apples from the slow cooker and set aside to cool. Otherwise, cook for an additional 2 to 3 hours (to finish cooking more quickly, set the slow cooker to high). The apples will simmer down nicely, while the beets will remain soft but should not be mushy.

Preparation and Storage for Baby

When cooled, puree the food in batches. Use a food processor to achieve a smooth texture and add water, formula, or breast milk as you continue to puree. You can also partially puree the apples and beets so that the food has some lumps to help baby make the transition to table foods. Using a slotted spoon, remove some of the beets and then spoon out some of the apples; set aside to offer as a finger food meal.

Store in the refrigerator for up to 3 days for babies.

To freeze, follow the stage two directions in "Freezing Homemade Baby Food" on page 28.

For the Family

Prior to reducing to a texture suitable for your baby, remove some of the beets and apples and set aside. Serve this mix as a delicious side dish.

❄ Freezes well, but you may see some ice crystals. Some separation may occur when thawed; mix to recombine.
🍎 B vitamins, including folate, and A and C, plus fiber and a little bit of iron and calcium

One of the great advantages of making your own homemade baby food is that you get to choose exactly what goes into it—which means you control the quality.

Black Beans and Sweet Potatoes

This is a "treasure" recipe; mash the sweet potatoes and leave the beans whole and let baby pick through the sweet potatoes to find the beans. Or mash the beans and add chunks of soft-cooked sweet potatoes. Either way you want to serve this, your baby will be happy to pick through her plate.

Age and Stage: (6) 8 months+ | Stage Two | Second Foods and Beyond
Slow Cooker Size: 4 to 6 quarts (3.8 to 5.7 l); oval

1 pound (455 g) dried black beans
2 large sweet potatoes
2 apples, such as McIntosh, cored, peeled, and diced (optional)
6 cups (1.4 l) cold water
¼ cup (40 g) minced onion (optional)
1 teaspoon garlic powder (optional)
½ teaspoon ground pepper (optional)
Cheddar cheese, shredded (optional)

> **Caution:** *Beans must be soaked for at least 5 hours and then boiled for 10 minutes prior to cooking them in a slow cooker. Legumes will concentrate and emit phytohaemagglutinin, which is a form of lectin that can be toxic at high levels. Soaking and boiling beans prior to slow cooking will prevent this potential health hazard. Note also that beans may cause baby to have some gassiness.*

1. Place the beans in a bowl, cover with water, and soak for at least 5 hours.
2. Drain the beans, transfer to a saucepan, cover with water, and boil for 10 minutes. Drain the water. Rinse the beans and pick through them for any debris.
3. Peel the sweet potatoes and chop into small but relatively uniform chunks.
4. Transfer the beans and sweet potatoes to the slow cooker. Add the apples (if using), water, and onion, garlic powder, and pepper (if using).
5. Cover and cook on low for 6 hours, checking after 3 hours and adding more water if needed. After 6 hours, check the texture of the sweet potatoes and beans. If the sweet potatoes and beans are both soft cooked, remove the food from the slow cooker and set aside to cool; discard liquid. Otherwise, cook for an additional 1 to 2 hours (to finish cooking more quickly, set the slow cooker to high). The apples will simmer down nicely, while the sweet potatoes and beans should remain soft but not mushy. If using, sprinkle a bit of shredded cheese over the mixture and stir to combine.

Preparation and Storage for Baby

When cooled, puree the food in batches. Use a food processor to achieve a smooth texture and add water, formula, or breast milk as you continue to puree. You can also partially puree so that the food has some lumps to help baby make the transition to table foods. Using a slotted spoon, remove some of the sweet potatoes and beans and then spoon out some of the apples; set aside to offer as a finger food meal.

Store in the refrigerator for up to 3 days for babies.

To freeze, follow the stage two directions in "Freezing Homemade Baby Food" on page 28.

For the Family

Prior to reducing to a texture suitable for your baby, remove some of the sweet potatoes and apples and set aside. Serve this mix—sprinkled with additional shredded cheddar cheese, if desired—as a delicious side dish.

❄ Freezes well, but you may see some ice crystals. Some separation may occur when thawed; mix to recombine. 🍎 B vitamins, including folate, and A and C, as well as fiber, iron, and calcium

Black Beans and Apples

This is another "treasure" recipe; leave the beans whole and let baby pick through them to find the apple chunks. Or mash the apples and leave the soft-cooked beans. Either way you want to serve this, your baby will be happy to pick through his plate.

Age and Stage: (6) 8 months+ | Stage Two | Second Foods and Beyond

Slow Cooker Size: 4 to 6 quarts (3.8 to 5.7 l); oval

8 ounces (225 g) dried black beans or 3 cans (15 ounces [425 g] each), not drained
5 large apples, such as McIntosh
3 cups (710 ml) cold water (1 cup [235 ml] if using canned beans)
½ teaspoon ground cinnamon (optional)

1. If using dried beans, place the beans in a bowl, cover with water, and soak for at least 5 hours.
2. Drain the beans, transfer to a saucepan, cover with water, and boil for 10 minutes. Drain the water. Rinse the beans and pick through them for any debris.
3. Peel and core the apples. Chop them into relatively uniform chunks.
4. Transfer the boiled or canned beans and the apples to the slow cooker. Add the water and cinnamon (if using). Stir to combine.
5. Cover and cook on low for 6 hours, checking after 3 hours and adding more water if needed. After 6 hours, check the texture of the beans. If they're soft, remove the food from the slow cooker and set aside to cool; discard liquid. Otherwise, cook for an additional 2 to 3 hours (to finish cooking more quickly, set the slow cooker to high). The apples will simmer down nicely, while the beans should remain soft but not mushy.

Preparation and Storage for Baby

Use a food processor to achieve a smooth texture and add water, formula, or breast milk as you continue to puree. You can also partially puree the apples and beans so that the food has some lumps to help baby make the transition to table foods. Using a slotted spoon, remove some of the beans and then spoon out some of the apples; set aside to offer as a finger food meal.

Store in the refrigerator for up to 3 days for babies.

To freeze, follow the stage two directions in "Freezing Homemade Baby Food" on page 28.

For the Family

Prior to reducing to a texture suitable for your baby, remove some of the beans and apples and set aside. Serve this mix as a delicious side dish.

Note that beans may cause baby to have some gassiness.

❄ Freezes well, but you may see some ice crystals. Some separation may occur when thawed; mix to recombine. B vitamins, including folate, and A and C, plus fiber and a little bit of iron and calcium

Butternut Squash with Apples

I love this recipe and my kids do too, even now that they are older. Whether you roast or slow-cook, the flavor combination of these two foods is fabulous.

Age and Stage: (6) 8 months+ | Stage Two | Second Foods and Beyond
Slow Cooker Size: 4 to 6 quarts (3.8 to 5.7 l); oval

> 1 butternut squash
> 5 large apples, such as McIntosh
> 1 cup (235 ml) cold water
> 2 tablespoons (28 ml) maple syrup
> ½ teaspoon ground cinnamon (optional)
> ½ teaspoon vanilla extract (optional)
> ½ teaspoon each sage, rosemary, and thyme (optional)

1. Wash and peel the butternut squash. Cut it in half and scoop out the seeds (set them aside to roast). Halve, core, and peel the apples. Roughly chop the squash and apples into relatively uniform chunks.
2. Transfer the squash and apples to the slow cooker. Add the water and maple syrup. If you'd like a sweeter dish, add the cinnamon and vanilla. If you'd like a more savory dish, add the herbs. Stir to combine.
3. Cover and cook on low for 4 to 6 hours, checking after 3 hours and adding more water if needed. After 4 to 6 hours, check the texture of the squash. If it's soft, remove the food from the slow cooker and set aside to cool. Otherwise, cook for an additional 2 to 3 hours (to finish cooking more quickly, set the slow cooker to high). The apples will cook down nicely, while the squash should remain soft but not overly mushy.

Preparation and Storage for Baby

Once cooled, puree the food in batches. Use a food processor to achieve a smooth texture and add water, formula, or breast milk as you continue to puree. You can also partially puree the squash and apples or use a masher so that the food has some lumps to help baby make the transition to table foods.

Store in the refrigerator for up to 3 days for babies.

To freeze, follow the stage two directions in "Freezing Homemade Baby Food" on page 28.

For the Family

Prior to reducing to a texture suitable for your baby, remove some of the squash and apples and set aside. Serve this mix as a delicious side dish or puree to a thin consistency and ladle over pork roast or chicken.

❄ Freezes well, but you may see some ice crystals. Some separation may occur when thawed; mix to recombine.
🍎 Vitamins A, C, and E, folate, fiber, and a little bit of iron, calcium, potassium, and magnesium

Butternut Squash with Peaches: Orange You Glad?

Peaches bring out the sweeter side of butternut squash, and when they're cooked together, the orange hue is delightful. Pair this wonderful mix with beets and apples, and let your baby or toddler finger paint during a meal. I know it's messy, but remember that babies and toddlers learn about food by taste, sight, and touch.

Age and Stage: (6) 8 months+ | Stage Two | Second Foods and Beyond
Slow Cooker Size: 4 to 6 quarts (3.8 to 5.7 l); oval

> 1 butternut squash
> 1 bag (1 pound [455 g]) frozen peaches or 2 pounds (907 g) fresh peaches
> 1 cup (235 ml) water

1. Wash and peel the butternut squash. Cut it in half and scoop out the seeds (set them aside to roast). Roughly chop the squash into relatively uniform chunks. If using fresh peaches, wash, halve, peel, and pit them. (You may leave the skin on if you will be mashing or pureeing so that no choking hazard is present.)
2. Transfer the squash and peaches to the slow cooker. Add the water. Stir to combine.
3. Cover and cook on low for 4 to 6 hours, checking after 3 hours and adding more water if needed. After 4 to 6 hours, check the texture of the squash. If it's soft, remove the food from the slow cooker and set aside to cool. Otherwise, cook for an additional 2 to 3 hours (to finish cooking more quickly, set the slow cooker to high).

Preparation and Storage for Baby

When cooled, puree the food in batches. Use a food processor to achieve a smooth texture and add water, formula, or breast milk as you continue to puree. You can also partially puree the squash and peaches so that the food has some lumps to help baby make the transition to table foods. Using a slotted spoon, remove some of the squash and then spoon out some of the peaches; set aside to offer as a finger food meal.

Store in the refrigerator for up to 3 days for babies.

To freeze, follow the stage two directions in "Freezing Homemade Baby Food" on page 28.

For the Family

Prior to reducing to a texture suitable for your baby, remove some of the squash and peaches and set aside. Serve this mix as a delicious side dish or puree to a thin consistency and ladle over pork roast or chicken.

❄ Freezes well, but you may see some ice crystals. Some separation may occur when thawed; mix to recombine. 🍎 Vitamins A, C, and E, fiber, and a little bit of iron, calcium, and potassium

Butternut Squash, Sweet Potatoes, and Apples

The ultimate in finger food and self-feeding fun, these three foods are great when slow-cooked and given to baby to feed himself. Both of my boys loved bowls full of a mix of different foods to pick through. Watch to see which food is your baby's favorite when you serve this.

Age and Stage: (6) 8 months+ | Stage Two | Second Foods and Beyond
Slow Cooker Size: 4 to 6 quarts (3.8 to 5.7 l); oval

  1 butternut squash
  4 sweet potatoes
  6 apples, such as McIntosh
  1 cup (235 ml) water

1. Wash and peel the butternut squash. Cut it in half and scoop out the seeds (set them aside to roast). Wash and peel the sweet potatoes. Wash, halve, core, and peel the apples. Roughly chop the squash, sweet potatoes, and apples into relatively uniform chunks.
2. Transfer the squash, sweet potatoes, and apples to the slow cooker. Add the water. Stir to combine.
3. Cover and cook on low for 4 to 6 hours, checking after 3 hours and adding more water if needed. After 4 to 6 hours, check the texture of the squash and sweet potatoes. If they're tender, remove the food from the slow cooker and set aside to cool. Otherwise, cook for an additional 2 to 3 hours (to finish cooking more quickly, set the slow cooker to high). The apples will simmer down nicely, while the squash should remain soft but not overly mushy and the sweet potatoes may stay a bit firm.

Preparation and Storage for Baby

When cooled, puree the food in batches. Use a food processor to achieve a smooth texture and add water, formula, or breast milk as you continue to puree. You can also partially puree the food so that the food has some lumps to help baby make the transition to table foods. Using a slotted spoon, remove some of the squash and sweet potatoes, then spoon out some of the apples; set aside to offer as a finger food meal.

Store in the refrigerator for up to 3 days for babies.

To freeze, follow the stage two directions in "Freezing Homemade Baby Food" on page 28.

For the Family

Prior to reducing to a texture suitable for your baby, remove some of the food and set aside. Serve this mix as a delicious side dish.

❄ Freezes well, but you may see some ice crystals. Some separation may occur when thawed; mix to recombine.
● Vitamins A, C, and E, fiber, and a little bit of iron, calcium, and potassium

Carrots and Black Beans

A colorful recipe that's so much fun for Halloween! You might want to skip the pureeing step in this recipe because the cooked carrots and black beans make perfect finger food for babies. Imagine a bowl of black beans and chunks of lovely orange carrots; it's good.

Age and Stage: (6) 8 months+ | Stage Two | Second Foods and Beyond
Slow Cooker Size: 4 to 6 quarts (3.8 to 5.7 l); oval

> 8 ounces (225 g) dried black beans
> 5 large carrots
> ¼ cup (40 g) minced onion
> 3 cups (710 ml) cold water
> 1 teaspoon ground pepper (optional)

1. Place the beans in a bowl, cover with water, and soak for at least 5 hours.
2. Drain the beans, transfer to a saucepan, cover with water, and boil for 10 minutes. Drain the water. Rinse the beans and pick through them for any debris.
3. Wash, peel, and roughly chop the carrots into relatively uniform chunks.
4. Transfer the beans and carrots to the slow cooker. Add the onion, water, and pepper (if using). Stir to combine.
5. Cover and cook on low for 6 hours, checking after 3 hours and adding more water if needed. After 6 hours, check the texture of the beans. If they're soft, remove the food from the slow cooker and set aside to cool; discard liquid. Otherwise, cook for an additional 1 to 2 hours (to finish cooking more quickly, set the slow cooker to high).

Preparation and Storage for Baby

When cooled, puree the food in batches, if desired. Use a food processor to achieve a smooth texture and add water, formula, or breast milk as you continue to puree. You can also partially puree the carrots and beans so that the food has some lumps to help baby make the transition to table foods. Using a slotted spoon, remove some of the beans and then spoon out some of the carrots; set aside to offer as a finger food meal.

Store in the refrigerator for up to 3 days for babies.

To freeze, follow the stage two directions in "Freezing Homemade Baby Food" on page 28.

For the Family

Prior to reducing to a texture suitable for your baby, remove some of the beans and carrots and set aside. Serve this mix stuffed into a burrito or over rice; add shredded pork or chicken and you have a great meal!

❄ Freezes well, but you may see some ice crystals. Some separation may occur when thawed; mix to recombine.
● B vitamins, including folate, and A and C, plus fiber, protein, and a little bit of iron and calcium

Lentils and Carrots with Apples

If you can get your kids to enjoy lentils, you will be able to take advantage of a food that is high in protein, iron, fiber, and folate. If at first you don't succeed, try, try again—or add more apples.

Age and Stage: (6) 8 months+ | Stage Two | Second Foods and Beyond
Slow Cooker Size: 4 to 6 quarts (3.8 to 5.7 l); oval

2 cups (384 g) dried red lentils
4 large carrots
3 large apples, such as McIntosh
¼ cup (40 g) minced onion (optional)
6 cups (1.4 l) cold water or sodium-free chicken or vegetable broth or a combination of water and broth
1 teaspoon ground pepper

1. Rinse the lentils and pick through them for debris. Wash and peel the carrots. Wash, halve, core, and peel the apples. Roughly chop the carrots and apples into relatively uniform chunks.
2. Transfer the lentils, carrots, and apples to the slow cooker. Add the onion (if using), water and/or broth, and pepper (if using). Stir to combine.
3. Cover and cook on low for 6 hours, checking after 3 hours and adding more water if needed. After 6 hours, check the texture of the lentils. If they're soft and melting and the carrots are soft as well, remove the food from the slow cooker and set aside to cool. Otherwise, cook for an additional 1 to 2 hours (to finish cooking more quickly, set the slow cooker to high). The apples will simmer down nicely, while the lentils should remain soft but not overly mushy.

Preparation and Storage for Baby

When cooled, puree the food in batches. Use a food processor to achieve a smooth texture and add water, formula, or breast milk as you continue to puree. You can also partially puree the food so that there are some lumps to help baby make the transition to table foods. Using a slotted spoon, remove some of the carrots and then spoon out some of the apples; set aside to offer as a finger food meal.

Store in the refrigerator for up to 3 days for babies.

To freeze, follow the stage two directions in "Freezing Homemade Baby Food" on page 28.

For the Family

Serve up this dish with warm crusty bread and cheese with a salad.

❄ Freezes well, but you may see some ice crystals. Some separation may occur when thawed; mix to recombine.
🍎 B vitamins, including folate, and C, as well as fiber, protein, and a little bit of iron and calcium

Lentils and Pumpkin (with Apples and Pears)

This combination is sweet rather than savory and is truly a flavorful meal for babies.

Age and Stage: (6) 8 months+ | Stage Two | Second Foods and Beyond
Slow Cooker Size: 4 to 6 quarts (3.8 to 5.7 l); oval

  2 cups (384 g) dried red lentils
  1 large apple, such as McIntosh (optional)
  2 pears, such as Anjou (optional)
  1 can (15 ounces [425 g]) pumpkin puree (not pumpkin pie mix)
  6 cups (1.4 l) cold water or sodium-free chicken or vegetable broth or a combination of water and broth
  1 teaspoon ground cinnamon (optional)
  1 teaspoon ground nutmeg (optional)

1. Rinse the lentils and pick through them for debris. Wash, halve, core, and peel the apple and pears (if using). Roughly chop the apple and pears into relatively uniform chunks.
2. Transfer the beans to the slow cooker. Add the pumpkin, apple, pears, and water and/or broth. Add the cinnamon and nutmeg (if using). Stir to combine.
3. Cover and cook on low for 6 to 8 hours, checking after 3 hours and adding more water if needed. After 6 to 8 hours, check the texture of the lentils. If they're soft and melting, remove the food from the slow cooker and set aside to cool. Otherwise, cook for an additional 1 to 2 hours (to finish cooking more quickly, set the slow cooker to high). The apple and pears will simmer down nicely, while the lentils should remain soft but not overly mushy.

Preparation and Storage for Baby

When cooled, puree the food in batches. Use a food processor to achieve a smooth texture and add water, formula, or breast milk as you continue to puree. You can also partially puree the foods so that there are some lumps to help baby make the transition to table foods.

  Store in the refrigerator for up to 3 days for babies.

  To freeze, follow the stage two directions in "Freezing Homemade Baby Food" on page 28.

For the Family

Serve up this dish as a side with roasted chicken and rice pilaf.

❄ Freezes well, but you may see some ice crystals. Some separation may occur when thawed; mix to recombine.
🍎 B vitamins, including folate, and A and C, as well as fiber, protein, and a little bit of iron and calcium

Orange Trio

One thing is certain: The veggies in this recipe are bright and orange. They're also bursting with vitamin A, which is important for good vision, bone growth, and supporting the immune system.

Age and Stage: (6) 8 months+ | Stage Two | Second Foods and Beyond
Slow Cooker Size: 4 to 6 quarts (3.8 to 5.7 l); oval

> 1 sugar/baking pumpkin (5 to 6 pounds [2.3 to 2.7 kg])
> 6 large carrots
> 4 large sweet potatoes
> 1 cup (235 ml) cold water or salt-free chicken or vegetable broth
> 1 teaspoon poultry seasoning (optional)
> ½ teaspoon ground ginger (optional)
> ½ teaspoon ground cinnamon (optional)

1. Wash and peel the pumpkin, carrots, and sweet potatoes and cut into relatively uniform chunks.
2. Transfer the carrots, sweet potatoes, and pumpkin to the slow cooker. Add the water or broth. If using the spices, add either the poultry seasoning or the ginger and cinnamon. Stir to combine.
3. Cover and cook on low for 6 hours, checking after 3 hours and adding more water if needed. After 6 hours, check the texture of the sweet potatoes and carrots. If they're soft, remove the food from the slow cooker and set aside to cool. Otherwise, cook for an additional 1 to 2 hours (to finish cooking more quickly, set the slow cooker to high). The pumpkin will cook faster than the sweet potatoes and carrots and will simmer down, while the sweet potatoes and carrots should remain soft but not overly mushy.

Preparation and Storage for Baby

When cooled, puree the food in batches. Use a food processor to achieve a smooth texture and add water, formula, or breast milk as you continue to puree. You can also partially puree the food so that there are some lumps to help baby make the transition to table foods. When possible, keep some of the sweet potatoes and carrots in their soft, chunky form so that baby can self-feed.

Store in the refrigerator for up to 3 days for babies.

To freeze, follow the stage two directions in "Freezing Homemade Baby Food" on page 28.

For the Family

Serve up this dish as a side with any type of protein and rice or potatoes.

❄ Freezes well, but you may see some ice crystals. Some separation may occur when thawed; mix to recombine.
● B vitamins, including folate, and A (a lot!), C, and E, plus fiber and a little bit of iron and calcium

Parsnips and Apples

This is one of my very favorite combinations. As an alternative to the slow cooker method described here, you could roast the parsnips and apples in the oven. Either way, the results will always be delicious!

Age and Stage: (6) 8 months+ | Stage Two | Second Foods and Beyond
Slow Cooker Size: 4 quarts (3.8 l); round

6 parsnips
4 large apples, such as McIntosh
1 tablespoon (15 ml) extra-virgin olive oil
½ teaspoon ground cinnamon (optional)

1. Wash the parsnips and apples. Peel the parsnips and halve, core, and peel the apples. Roughly chop the parsnips and apples into relatively uniform chunks.
2. Pour the olive oil in the slow cooker and add the parsnips and apples. Add the cinnamon, if using. Stir to combine.
3. Cover and cook on low for 6 hours, stirring frequently to keep the food from sticking. Check the texture of the parsnips. If they're soft, remove the food from the slow cooker and set aside to cool. Otherwise, cook for an additional 1 to 2 hours (to finish cooking more quickly, set the slow cooker to high). The apples will cook faster than the parsnips.

Preparation and Storage for Baby

When cooled, puree the food in batches. Use a food processor to achieve a smooth texture and add water, formula, or breast milk as you continue to puree. You can also partially puree the food so that there are some lumps to help baby make the transition to table foods. When possible, keep some of the apples and parsnips in their soft, chunky form so that baby can self-feed.

Store in the refrigerator for up to 3 days for babies.

To freeze, follow the stage two directions in "Freezing Homemade Baby Food" on page 28.

For the Family

Serve up this dish as a side with any type of protein and rice or potatoes.

❋ Freezes well, but you may see some ice crystals. Some separation may occur when thawed; mix to recombine.
🍎 B vitamins, including folate, and A, C, and E, plus fiber and a little bit of iron and calcium

Parsnips, Carrots, and Pears

This is a fabulous mix of root veggies and the sweet taste of pears; your baby, toddler, and even high schooler (okay, maybe not your high schooler because they tend to not like anything at all) will love this combination!

Age and Stage: (6) 8 months+ | Stage Two | Second Foods and Beyond
Slow Cooker Size: 4 quarts (3.8 l); round

6 parsnips
6 carrots
2 pears
1 tablespoon (15 ml) extra-virgin olive oil
¼ cup (40 g) minced onion
½ teaspoon dried sage (optional)
½ teaspoon dried rosemary (optional)
½ teaspoon dried thyme (optional)
½ cup (120 ml) sodium-free vegetable or chicken broth

1. Wash the parsnips, carrots, and pears. Peel the parsnips and carrots. Halve, core, and peel the pears. Roughly chop the parsnips and carrots into relatively uniform chunks. Quarter the pears.
2. Pour the olive oil in the slow cooker and add the parsnips and carrots. Top with the pears and onion. Add the sage, rosemary, and thyme, if using. Pour in the broth and stir to combine.
3. Cover and cook on low for 7 hours, stirring frequently to keep the food from sticking. Check the texture of the parsnips and carrots. If they're soft, remove the food from the slow cooker and set aside to cool. Otherwise, cook for an additional 1 to 2 hours (to finish cooking more quickly, set the slow cooker to high). The pears will cook faster than the parsnips and carrots and will almost disappear altogether.

Preparation and Storage for Baby

When cooled, puree the food in batches. Use a food processor to achieve a smooth texture and add water, formula, or breast milk as you continue to puree. You can also partially puree the food so that there are some lumps to help baby make the transition to table foods. When possible, keep some of the parsnips and carrots in their soft, chunky form so that baby can self-feed.

Store in the refrigerator for up to 3 days for babies.

To freeze, follow the stage two directions in "Freezing Homemade Baby Food" on page 28.

For the Family

Serve up this dish as a side with any type of protein and rice or potatoes. Or puree and turn the recipe into soup; just add more broth as you puree.

❄ Freezes well, but you may see some ice crystals. Some separation may occur when thawed; mix to recombine.
🍎 B vitamins, including folate, and A, C, and E, plus fiber and a little bit of iron and calcium

Parsnips and Pears

Nutty and sweet, these two flavors make a great combination that can be used as a dip for finger foods. You can also mix the puree into meats.

Age and Stage: (6) 8 months+ | Stage Two | Second Foods and Beyond
Slow Cooker Size: 4 quarts (3.8 l); round

6 parsnips
6 pears
1 teaspoon ground cinnamon (optional)
½ cup (120 ml) water

1. Wash the parsnips and pears. Peel the parsnips. Halve, core, and peel the pears. Roughly chop the parsnips into thin coins. Quarter the pears.
2. Transfer the parsnips to the slow cooker and then place the pears on top. Add the cinnamon, if using. Pour in the water and stir to combine.
3. Cover and cook on low for 5 hours, stirring frequently to keep the food from sticking. Check the texture of the parsnips. If they're soft, remove the food from the slow cooker and set aside to cool. Otherwise, cook for an additional 1 hour (to finish cooking more quickly, set the slow cooker to high). The pears will cook down faster than the parsnips and will seem to disappear altogether.

Preparation and Storage for Baby

When cooled, puree the food in batches. Use a food processor to achieve a smooth texture and add water, formula, or breast milk as you continue to puree. You can also partially puree the food so that there are some lumps to help baby make the transition to table foods. When possible, keep some of the parsnips in their soft, chunky form so that baby can self-feed.

Store in the refrigerator for up to 3 days for babies.

To freeze, follow the stage two directions in "Freezing Homemade Baby Food" on page 28.

For the Family

If you've created a nice thin puree, this is a really great mix to use for chicken or pork; spoon over chicken breasts or boneless pork chops and then bake as you typically would.

❄ Freezes well, but you may see some ice crystals. Some separation may occur when thawed; mix to recombine.
🍎 B vitamins, including folate, and C, E, and K, plus fiber and a little bit of iron and calcium

Peaches and Pumpkin

Another great combination of flavors, this recipe is great as a sauce and a dip, too.

Age and Stage: (6) 8 months+ | Stage Two | Second Foods and Beyond
Slow Cooker Size: 4 quarts (3.8 l); oval

1 sugar/baking pumpkin (5 to 6 pounds [2.3 to 2.7 kg])
8 fresh peaches or 1 bag (1 pound [455 g]) frozen peaches
1 teaspoon ground cinnamon (optional)
1 teaspoon vanilla extract (optional)
½ cup (120 ml) water

1. Wash the pumpkin and the peaches, if using fresh. Peel the pumpkin and scoop out the seeds (set them aside to roast later). If using fresh peaches, halve, pit, and peel them. Cut into quarters. Roughly chop the pumpkin.
2. Transfer the pumpkin to the slow cooker. Add the fresh or frozen peaches on top. Add the cinnamon and vanilla, if using. Stir to combine. Add the water.
3. Cover and cook on low for 5 hours, stirring frequently to keep the food from sticking. Check the texture of the pumpkin. If it's soft, remove the food from the slow cooker and set aside to cool. Otherwise, cook for an additional 1 hour (to finish cooking more quickly, set the slow cooker to high). The peaches will cook down faster than the pumpkin and will seem to disappear altogether.

Preparation and Storage for Baby

When cooled, puree the food in batches. Use a food processor to achieve a smooth texture and add water, formula, or breast milk as you continue to puree. You can also mash or partially puree the food so that there are some lumps to help baby make the transition to table foods. When possible, keep some of the pumpkin in its soft, chunky form so that baby can self-feed.

Store in the refrigerator for up to 3 days for babies.

To freeze, follow the stage two directions in "Freezing Homemade Baby Food" on page 28.

For the Family

I like to let this recipe simmer down into a butter. You might want to take half for baby food and then continue to cook the remaining half to create a butter.

❄ Freezes well, but you may see some ice crystals. Some separation may occur when thawed; mix to recombine.
🍎 B vitamins, including folate, and C, E, and K, plus fiber and a little bit of iron and calcium

Peaches, Pears, and Acorn Squash

Acorn squash is aptly named due to its shape and the way the stem grows. When my kids learned about acorn squash, they wanted to take their squash and feed it to the squirrels.

Age and Stage: (6) 8 months+ | Stage Two | Second Foods and Beyond
Slow Cooker Size: 4 to 6 quarts (3.8 to 5.7 l); oval

1 acorn squash
8 fresh peaches or 1 bag (1 pound [455 g]) frozen peaches
6 fresh pears
1 teaspoon ground cinnamon (optional)
1 teaspoon ground ginger (optional)
1 teaspoon vanilla extract (optional)
½ cup (120 ml) water

1. Wash the squash, peaches (if using fresh), and pears. Peel the squash and scoop out the seeds (set them aside to roast later). Roughly chop. If using fresh peaches, halve, pit, and peel them. Cut into quarters. Halve, core, peel, and quarter the pears.
2. Transfer the squash and pears to the slow cooker. Add the fresh or frozen peaches on top. Add the cinnamon, ginger, and vanilla, if using. Stir to combine. Add the water.
3. Cover and cook on low for 5 hours, stirring frequently to keep the food from sticking. Check the texture of the squash. If it's soft, remove the food from the slow cooker and set aside to cool. Otherwise, cook for an additional 1 hour (to finish cooking more quickly, set the slow cooker to high). The peaches will cook down faster than the squash and pears and will seem to disappear altogether.

Preparation and Storage for Baby

When cooled, puree the food in batches. Use a food processor to achieve a smooth texture and add water, formula, or breast milk as you continue to puree. You can also mash or partially puree the food so that there are some lumps to help baby make the transition to table foods. When possible, keep some of the squash and pears in their soft, chunky form so that baby can self-feed.

Store in the refrigerator for up to 3 days for babies.

To freeze, follow the stage two directions in "Freezing Homemade Baby Food" on page 28.

For the Family

This is such a great-tasting dish that you can eat it as a side. To make an updated version of shepherd's pie, mix it with cooked rice and cooked ground turkey, then spread in a baking dish and add an additional layer of the puree on top. Bake at 350°F (180°C) for 25 minutes.

❄ Freezes well, but you may see some ice crystals. Some separation may occur when thawed; mix to recombine.
🍎 B vitamins, including folate, and C, E, and K, plus fiber and a little bit of iron and calcium

Pumpkin and Apples

If you like the flavors of fall, take your kids to an orchard and pumpkin picking, too; then go home and make this dish.

Age and Stage: (6) 8 months+ | Stage Two | Second Foods and Beyond
Slow Cooker Size: 4 quarts (3.8 l); oval

1 sugar/baking pumpkin (5 to 6 pounds [2.3 to 2.7 kg])
10 apples, such as McIntosh or Granny Smith
½ teaspoon ground cinnamon (optional)
½ teaspoon ground nutmeg (optional)
1 teaspoon vanilla extract (optional)
½ cup (120 ml) water

1. Wash the pumpkin and apples. Peel the pumpkin and scoop out the seeds (set them aside to roast later). Halve, core, and peel the apples. Roughly chop the apples and pumpkin.
2. Transfer the pumpkin to the slow cooker and add the apples on top. Add the cinnamon, nutmeg, and vanilla, if using. Stir to combine. Add the water.
3. Cover and cook on low for 5 hours, stirring frequently to keep the food from sticking. Check the texture of the pumpkin. If it's soft, remove the food from the slow cooker and set aside to cool. Otherwise, cook for an additional 1 hour (to finish cooking more quickly, set the slow cooker to high). The apples will cook down faster than the pumpkin and will seem to disappear altogether.

Preparation and Storage for Baby

When cooled, puree the food in batches. Use a food processor to achieve a smooth texture and add water, formula, or breast milk as you continue to puree. You can also mash or partially puree the food so that there are some lumps to help baby make the transition to table foods. When possible, keep some of the pumpkin in its soft, chunky form so that baby can self-feed.

Store in the refrigerator for up to 3 days for babies.

To freeze, follow the stage two directions in "Freezing Homemade Baby Food" on page 28.

For the Family

Simmer the mixture into a butter and fill jelly jars to gift to friends and family. Or spread the puree over chicken or pork and roast, or serve as a side dish with turkey, chicken, or pork. If making stuffing, add ½ cup of the puree to your regular recipe, and then toss in a handful of raisins, too!

❄ Freezes well, but you may see some ice crystals. Some separation may occur when thawed; mix to recombine.
● Vitamins A, B, C, and E, fiber, and a little bit of iron and calcium

Pumpkin, Pears, and Apples

These three fruits make a great centerpiece for a fall or holiday table. Why not display them before you cook them?

Age and Stage: (6) 8 months+ | Stage Two | Second Foods and Beyond
Slow Cooker Size: 4 to 6 quarts (3.8 to 5.7 l); oval

1 sugar/baking pumpkin (5 to 6 pounds [2.3 to 2.7 kg])
10 apples, such as McIntosh or Granny Smith
10 fresh pears
½ cup (120 ml) water

1. Wash the pumpkin, apples, and pears. Halve the pumpkin and scoop out the seeds (set them aside to roast later). Peel the pumpkin and roughly chop. Halve, core, peel, and roughly chop the apples. Halve, core, peel, and quarter the pears.
2. Transfer the pumpkin to the slow cooker and add the pears and apples on top. Add the water.
3. Cover and cook on low for 5 hours, stirring frequently to keep the food from sticking. Check the texture of the pumpkin. If it's soft, remove the food from the slow cooker and set aside to cool. Otherwise, cook for an additional 1 hour (to finish cooking more quickly, set the slow cooker to high). The pears and apples will cook down faster than the pumpkin and will seem to disappear altogether.

Preparation and Storage for Baby

When cooled, puree the food in batches. Use a food processor to achieve a smooth texture and add water, formula, or breast milk as you continue to puree. You can also mash or partially puree the food so that there are some lumps to help baby make the transition to table foods. When possible, keep some of the pumpkin in its soft, chunky form so that baby can self-feed.

Store in the refrigerator for up to 3 days for babies.

To freeze, follow the stage two directions in "Freezing Homemade Baby Food" on page 28.

For the Family

Serve as a side dish, mix the puree with yogurt or oatmeal, or blend it into a smoothie.

❄ Freezes well, but you may see some ice crystals. Some separation may occur when thawed; mix to recombine.
🍎 B vitamins, including folate, and C and E, plus fiber and a little bit of iron and calcium

Root Veggie Trio with Apples and Fennel

These lovely root veggies receive an extra depth of flavor and sweetness when you add in apples and fennel. While this is a great recipe for the slow cooker, you should also try roasting these together sometime!

Age and Stage: (6) 8 months+ | Stage Two | Second Foods and Beyond
Slow Cooker Size: 4 to 6 quarts (3.8 to 5.7 l); oval

1 pound (455 g) carrots
1 pound (455 g) parsnips
1 pound (455 g) turnips
6 large apples, such as McIntosh
1 bulb fennel
¼ cup (60 ml) extra-virgin olive oil
1 cup (235 ml) cold water

1. Wash all of the vegetables and the apples and fennel. Peel the carrots, parsnips, and turnips. Halve, core, and peel the apples. Dice the vegetables and apples into uniform pieces.
2. Trim the fennel stalks and cut the bulb in half and then into quarters. Transfer to a covered container and set aside in the refrigerator.
3. Transfer the vegetables and apples to the slow cooker. Add the oil and stir to combine.
4. Cover and cook on low for 6 hours or on high for 4 hours. After the first hour, add the water. Check again after 3 hours and add additional water if needed. When 30 minutes of cooking time remain, add the fennel and stir. The root vegetables will simmer down nicely, but not so much that they are a watery mess. Remove the food from the slow cooker and set aside to cool.

Preparation and Storage for Baby

When cooled, puree the food in batches. Use a food processor to achieve a smooth texture and add water, formula, or breast milk as you continue to puree. You can also partially puree so that the food has some lumps to help baby make the transition to table foods. When possible, keep some of the vegetables in their soft, chunky form so that baby can self-feed.

Store in the refrigerator for up to 3 days for babies.

To freeze, follow the stage two directions in "Freezing Homemade Baby Food" on page 28.

For the Family

Serve this recipe as a delicious side dish. Prior to reducing to a texture suitable for your baby, remove some of the veggies and apples and set aside. Add these reserved portions to salads or reduce to a soup.

❄ Freezes well, but some separation may occur when thawed; mix to recombine.
🍎 Vitamins A, B, C, and E, iron, potassium, calcium, and magnesium

Spaghetti Squash and Carrots

When your kids are older, make spaghetti squash for them and let them use a fork to scrape the squash into "spaghetti." Then let them decide what type of sauce they want to use. The more you involve your kids in preparing and cooking foods, the better choices they will make as they grow up.

Age and Stage: (6) 8 months+ | Stage Two | Second Foods and Beyond
Slow Cooker Size: 4 to 6 quarts (3.8 to 5.7 l); oval

1 spaghetti squash (4 to 6 pounds [1.8 to 2.7 kg])
1 pound (455 g) carrots
½ cup (120 ml) water
2 tablespoons (28 ml) extra-virgin olive oil
1 tablespoon (10 g) minced garlic (optional)
1 teaspoon ground pepper (optional)

1. Wash the spaghetti squash and carrots. Cut the squash in half and scoop out the seeds. Peel the carrots and chop into thin coins.
2. Pour the water and oil into the slow cooker. Place the squash halves cut side down in the slow cooker. Add the carrots around the squash. Add the garlic and pepper, if using.
3. Cover and cook on low for 5 hours. Check the texture of the squash. The shell will begin to soften and seem to cave in when the squash is soft cooked. If the squash is done but the carrots aren't yet tender, remove the squash from the slow cooker and set aside to cool. Cook either the carrots alone or both the squash and carrots for an additional 1 hour (to finish cooking more quickly, set the slow cooker to high). Remove the carrots and squash from the slow cooker and set aside in separate bowls to cool.

Preparation and Storage for Baby

When cooled, drag a fork over the flesh of the spaghetti squash and scrape it out into a bowl. Puree the carrots and squash together in batches. Use a food processor to achieve a smooth texture and add water, formula, or breast milk as you continue to puree. You can also mash or partially puree the food so that there are some lumps to help baby make the transition to table foods. When possible, keep some of the squash and carrots in their soft, chunky form so that baby can self-feed.

You can serve the squash to babies without pureeing it; just be sure that the strands are an appropriate size so no choking hazard is present.

Store in the refrigerator for up to 3 days for babies.

To freeze, follow the stage two directions in "Freezing Homemade Baby Food" on page 28.

For the Family

Replace pasta with the spaghetti squash and serve it with sauce, meatballs, and carrots.

❄ Freezes well, but you may see some ice crystals. Some separation may occur when thawed; mix to recombine.
🍎 Vitamins A, C, and E, fiber, and a little bit of iron and calcium

Summer Squash with Apples

Sometimes when you make your own baby food, you come up with combinations that seem crazy but are really tasty.

Age and Stage: (6) 8 months+ | Stage Two | Second Foods and Beyond
Slow Cooker Size: 4 to 6 quarts (3.8 to 5.7 l); round

3 zucchini squash
3 yellow/crooked neck squash
6 apples, such as McIntosh or Granny Smith
½ cup (120 ml) water
½ teaspoon dried basil (optional)
½ teaspoon dried rosemary (optional)
½ teaspoon dried oregano (optional)
Pinch of garlic powder (optional

1. Wash the squash and apples. Peel the squash and cut into slices. Halve, core, and peel the apples. Chop into pieces.
2. Transfer the squash to the slow cooker. Add the apples and water. If using, add the basil, rosemary, oregano, and garlic powder. Stir to combine.
3. Cover and cook on low for 3 to 4 hours, checking frequently (squash and apples cook rather quickly). Remove the food from the slow cooker and set aside to cool.

Preparation and Storage for Baby

When cooled, puree the mixture in batches. Use a food processor to achieve a smooth texture and add water, formula, or breast milk as you continue to puree. You can also mash or partially puree the food so that there are some lumps to help baby make the transition to table foods. When possible, keep some of the squash and apples in their soft, chunky form so that baby can self-feed.

Store in the refrigerator for up to 3 days for babies.

To freeze, follow the stage two directions in "Freezing Homemade Baby Food" on page 28.

For the Family

This dish makes a great side for barbecue chicken.

❄ Freezes well, but you may see some ice crystals. Some separation may occur when thawed; mix to recombine.
🍎 Vitamins A, B, C, and E, fiber, and a little bit of iron and calcium

Sweet Potatoes with Spiced Pears

Sweet potatoes and pears are great finger foods separately. When you slow-cook these together, the flavors meld nicely and your kids will say, "We told you to cook them together in the big black pot!"

Age and Stage: (6) 8 months+ | Stage Two | Second Foods and Beyond
Slow Cooker Size: 4 to 6 quarts (3.8 to 5.7 l); oval

> 8 sweet potatoes
> 8 pears
> ½ cup (120 ml) water
> 1 teaspoon ground cinnamon (optional)

1. Wash the sweet potatoes and pears. Peel the sweet potatoes and cut into chunks. Halve, core, and peel the pears. Chop into quarters.
2. Transfer the sweet potatoes and pears to the slow cooker. Add the water. Add the cinnamon, if using. Stir to combine.
3. Cover and cook on low for 4 to 5 hours. Check the texture of the sweet potatoes. The pears will cook faster than the sweet potatoes. If desired, remove the pears and allow the sweet potatoes to continue to cook until tender. Remove the food from the slow cooker and set aside to cool.

Preparation and Storage for Baby

When cooled, puree sweet potatoes and pears together in batches. Use a food processor to achieve a smooth texture and add water, formula, or breast milk as you continue to puree. You can also mash or partially puree the food so that there are some lumps to help baby make the transition to table foods. When possible, keep some of the sweet potatoes and pears in their soft, chunky form so that baby can self-feed.

Store in the refrigerator for up to 3 days for babies.

To freeze, follow the stage two directions in "Freezing Homemade Baby Food" on page 28.

For the Family

If you have leftover sweet potatoes and spiced pears, you can make minisoufflés in a muffin pan. Combine 1 cup (220 g) of the pureed sweet potatoes and pears mix, 1 egg, ¼ cup (60 ml) milk, and ½ teaspoon vanilla extract. Spoon into a greased muffin pan and bake at 350°F (180°C) for 15 to 20 minutes. The minisoufflés will be done when the tops are springy to the touch or when a toothpick inserted into a soufflé comes out clean.

❄ Freezes well, but you may see some ice crystals. Some separation may occur when thawed; mix to recombine.
🍎 Vitamins A, B, C, and E, fiber, and a little bit of iron and calcium

Sweet Potatoes, Peaches, and Apples

Sweet potatoes, peaches, and apples are great when baked together, but they are also amazing when you slow-cook them together.

Age and Stage: (6) 8 months+ | Stage Two | Second Foods and Beyond
Slow Cooker Size: 4 to 6 quarts (3.8 to 5.7 l); oval

8 sweet potatoes
10 apples, such as McIntosh or Granny Smith
4 fresh ripe peaches or 2 cups (500 g) frozen sliced or diced peaches
½ cup (120 ml) water
1 teaspoon ground cinnamon (optional)
½ teaspoon vanilla extract (optional)

1. Wash the sweet potatoes, apples, and peaches (if using fresh). Peel and then chop the potatoes into chunks. Halve, core, peel, and roughly chop the apples. Halve, pit, peel, and roughly chop the peaches.
2. Transfer the sweet potatoes to the slow cooker. Add the apples, fresh or frozen peaches, and water. If using, add the cinnamon and vanilla. Stir to combine.
3. Cover and cook on low for 4 to 5 hours. Check the texture of the sweet potatoes. The apples and peaches will cook faster than the sweet potatoes. If necessary, remove the apples and peaches and allow the sweet potatoes to continue to cook until tender. Remove the food from the slow cooker and set aside to cool.

Preparation and Storage for Baby

Once cooled, puree the apples, peaches, and sweet potatoes together in batches. Use a food processor to achieve a smooth texture and add water, formula, or breast milk as you continue to puree. You can also mash or partially puree the food so that there are some lumps to help baby make the transition to table foods. When possible, keep some of the apples, peaches, and sweet potatoes in their soft, chunky form so that baby can self-feed.

Store in the refrigerator for up to 3 days for babies.

To freeze, follow the stage two directions in "Freezing Homemade Baby Food" on page 28.

For the Family

Serve as a side dish. Or take 3 cups (675 g) of the puree and add 4 cups (950 ml) of chicken or vegetable broth, blend and warm together in a saucepan, and it's soup!

❋ Freezes well, but you may see some ice crystals. Some separation may occur when thawed; mix to recombine.
🍎 Vitamins A, B, C, and E, fiber, and a little bit of iron and calcium

Sweet Potatoes and Peaches

Sweet potatoes and peaches—a tasty and beautiful orange mess that will drip through your little one's fingers while you try to remember that touch is just as important as taste when feeding your child.

Age and Stage: (6) 8 months+ | Stage Two | Second Foods and Beyond
Slow Cooker Size: 4 to 6 quarts (3.8 to 5.7 l); oval

8 sweet potatoes
8 fresh peaches or 1 bag (1 pound [455 g]) frozen peaches
½ cup (120 ml) water
1 teaspoon ground cinnamon (optional)

1. Wash the sweet potatoes and peaches, if using fresh. Peel the sweet potatoes and cut into chunks. Halve, pit, and peel the fresh peaches, then cut into quarters.
2. Transfer the sweet potatoes and fresh or frozen peaches to the slow cooker. Add the water and cinnamon, if using. Stir to combine.
3. Cover and cook on low for 4 to 5 hours. Check the texture of the sweet potatoes. The peaches will cook faster than the sweet potatoes. If necessary, remove the peaches and allow the sweet potatoes to continue to cook until tender. Remove the food from the slow cooker and set aside to cool.

Preparation and Storage for Baby

When cooled, puree the sweet potatoes and peaches together in batches. Use a food processor to achieve a smooth texture and add water, formula, or breast milk as you continue to puree. You can also mash or partially puree the food so that there are some lumps to help baby make the transition to table foods. When possible, keep some of the sweet potatoes and peaches in their soft, chunky form so that baby can self-feed.

Store in the refrigerator for up to 3 days for babies.

To freeze, follow the stage two directions in "Freezing Homemade Baby Food" on page 28.

For the Family

Serve as a tasty side dish with chicken or pork; add to a smoothie.

❄ Freezes well, but you may see some ice crystals. Some separation may occur when thawed; mix to recombine.
🍎 Vitamins A, B, C, and E, fiber, and a little bit of iron and calcium

Potatoes and Carrots

This recipe uses purple potatoes to create a lovely, colorful side dish for the family and food for baby. This should really be served as finger food so that baby can practice her fine-motor skills. Many times when I served my boys this dish and others like it, I would give them a big spoon to practice their scooping skills.

Age and Stage: (6) 8 months+ | Stage Two | Second Foods and Beyond
Slow Cooker Size: 4 to 6 quarts (3.8 to 5.7 l); oval

1 pound (455 g) carrots
2 bags (24 to 28 ounces [680 to 794 g] each) small purple potatoes
1 tablespoon (15 g) extra-virgin olive oil
1 teaspoon minced garlic

1. Wash the carrots and potatoes. Peel the carrots. Dice the carrots and potatoes as uniformly as possible.
2. Transfer the vegetables to the slow cooker. Add the oil and garlic and stir to combine.
3. Cover and cook on low for 5 hours. Remove the food from the slow cooker and set aside to cool.

Preparation and Storage for Baby

When cooled, puree the food in batches. Use a food processor to achieve a smooth texture and add water, formula, or breast milk as you continue to puree. You can also mash or partially puree so that the food has some lumps to help baby make the transition to table foods. This is great to serve in soft, chunky form so that baby can self-feed.

Store in the refrigerator for up to 3 days for babies.

To freeze, follow the stage two directions in "Freezing Homemade Baby Food" on page 28.

For the Family

Toss a portion on a small baking sheet and drizzle with extra-virgin olive oil (or a rosemary-infused extra-virgin olive oil) and balsamic vinegar; broil for 15 minutes.

❄ Freezes well, but potato puree is known to separate; mix to recombine
🍎 Vitamins A, B, C, and E, fiber, iron, potassium, calcium, and magnesium

Tasty Herbed Root Veggies

I like to slow-cook this recipe using purple potatoes or sweet potatoes. Here, I have used sweet potatoes, but you use the ones that you prefer. Don't let this cook to the point of total mush; this is a great recipe for babies to practice self-feeding, and it's colorful.

Age and Stage: (6) 8 months+ | Stage Two | Second Foods and Beyond
Slow Cooker Size: 4 to 6 quarts (3.8 to 5.7 l); oval

1 pound (455 g) carrots
1 pound (455 g) parsnips
3 medium sweet potatoes
¼ cup (60 ml) water
1 tablespoon (15 ml) extra-virgin olive oil
½ teaspoon dried rosemary
½ teaspoon dried oregano
½ teaspoon dried thyme
½ teaspoon ground pepper

1. Wash all of the vegetables. Peel and dice the carrots, parsnips, and sweet potatoes as uniformly as possible.
2. Transfer the vegetables to the slow cooker. Pour in the water and oil. Add the rosemary, oregano, thyme, and pepper and stir to combine.
3. Cover and cook on low for 4 to 5 hours, stirring after the first hour. The root vegetables will simmer down nicely, but not so much that they are a watery mess. Remove the food from the slow cooker and set aside to cool.

Preparation and Storage for Baby

When cooled, puree the food in batches. Use a food processor to achieve a smooth texture and add water, formula, or breast milk as you continue to puree. You can also mash or partially puree so that the foods have some lumps to help baby make the transition to table foods. This is great to serve in soft, chunky form so that baby can self-feed.

Store in the refrigerator for up to 3 days for babies.

To freeze, follow the stage two directions in "Freezing Homemade Baby Food" on page 28.

For the Family

Serve these vegetables as a delicious side dish. Prior to reducing to a texture suitable for your baby, remove some of the veggies and set aside. Add these reserved portions to salads or reduce to a soup.

❄ Freezes well. 🍎 Vitamins A, B, C, and E, fiber, iron, potassium, calcium, and magnesium

If your baby is six months old or older and has been eating solid foods for two weeks or more without tummy trouble, you can begin flavoring your homemade baby food with herbs and spices, which add flavor without salt or sugar.

Fifteen "Beyond Applesauce" Recipes

Most of baby's diet between 6 and 12 months old consists of fruits and vegetables with some grain and protein, too. The following "beyond applesauce" recipes offer interesting variety and extra nutrition, and they're sure to please babies, toddlers, and big kids alike.

In several of the recipes, I've given you a choice of using either water or apple juice. Be aware that offering your baby juice as a drink, in a bottle or a sippy cup, isn't a good idea. Juice is high in sugar and doesn't offer the fiber and nutrition of whole fruit, so juice as a drink is just not needed in baby's diet. However, adding a bit of juice to a full recipe isn't a bad thing to do. Your baby won't be drinking or eating the full amount of juice that you add to the recipe. Still, the choice to add juice, or even to cut it down by half, is entirely yours.

Finally, please note that none of the recipes in this chapter contain foods that are considered to be allergenic. However, you should always work with your pediatrician to ensure that foods are appropriate for your baby.

Apples and Blueberries

This is a great recipe that lets babies experience the wonder of superfoods as well as the colors of foods as they naturally occur. If you're feeling brave, offer your baby a bowl of oatmeal and a bowl of this sauce, and let him scoop this sauce into the oatmeal. Of course, you can offer a spoon for this, but hands and fingers will surely work better.

Age and Stage: 6 to 8 months+ | Stage One to Two | Second Foods and Beyond
Slow Cooker Size: 4 to 6 quarts (3.8 to 5.7 l); oval

10 apples, such as McIntosh
3 pints (870 g) fresh blueberries or 1 bag (1 pound [455 g]) frozen blueberries
1 teaspoon vanilla extract

1. Wash the apples and blueberries, if using fresh. Pick through the blueberries and discard any stems or debris. Halve, core, peel, and dice the apples.
2. Transfer the fruit to the slow cooker. Add the vanilla and stir to combine.
3. Cover and cook on low for 5 hours. Let the sauce cool in the slow cooker.

Preparation and Storage for Baby

When cooled, puree the sauce in batches. Use a handheld mixer or immersion blender and mix right in the slow cooker, or use a food processor to achieve a smoother texture. For babies, use water, formula, or breast milk as you continue to puree. You can also mash or partially puree the sauce and try to get some lumps, but this recipe will simmer down to a fairly smooth texture.

Store in the refrigerator for up to 3 days for babies.

To freeze, follow the stage two directions in "Freezing Homemade Baby Food" on page 28.

For the Family

Brush the puree on baby back ribs and bake them in the oven prior to grilling, or mix into yogurt and oatmeal or other breakfast cereals. It's great for spreading on biscuits, pancakes, and toast.

❄ Freezes well, but you will probably see some ice crystals due to the high water content of the apples and blueberries; mix to recombine.   🍎 Vitamins A, C, and E, fiber, iron, potassium, and calcium

Apples and Pears

If you cook this for the minimum time, the apples and pears will be soft enough to serve as finger foods.

Age and Stage: 6 to 8 months+ | Stage One to Two | Second Foods and Beyond

Slow Cooker Size: 4 to 6 quarts (3.8 to 5.7 l); oval

2 pounds (907 g) apples, such as Granny Smith, Gala, or Braeburn

1 pound (455 g) Anjou pears

1 teaspoon vanilla extract

1 teaspoon ground cinnamon

½ teaspoon ground cardamom

1. Wash the apples and pears. Halve, core, peel, and dice the apples and pears.
2. Transfer the fruit to the slow cooker. Add the vanilla, cinnamon, and cardamom. Stir to combine.
3. Cover and cook on low for 6 to 8 hours. Let the sauce cool in the slow cooker.

Preparation and Storage for Baby

When cooled, puree the sauce in batches. Use a handheld mixer or immersion blender and mix right in the slow cooker, or use a food processor to achieve a smoother texture. For babies, use water, formula, or breast milk as you continue to puree. You can also mash or partially puree the sauce and try to get some lumps, but this recipe will simmer down to a fairly smooth texture.

Store in the refrigerator for up to 3 days for babies.

To freeze, follow the stage two directions in "Freezing Homemade Baby Food" on page 28.

For the Family

This makes a great sauce for grilling chicken or pork and, of course, for spreading on biscuits and pancakes or mixing into cereal or oatmeal.

❊ Freezes well, but you will probably see some ice crystals due to the high water content of the apples and pears; mix to recombine.　🍎 Vitamins B_6, C, and E, fiber, iron, potassium, and calcium

Spiced Apple Pumpkin Sauce

This recipe highlights the favorite flavors of fall. My kids would willingly eat most of the meals I made in the fall because I would tell them that these were "fall" foods that the scarecrows and woodland creatures loved.

Age and Stage: 6 to 8 months+ | Stage One to Two | Second Foods and Beyond
Slow Cooker Size: 4 to 6 quarts (3.8 to 5.7 l); oval

3 pounds (1.4 kg) apples, such as Granny Smith
1 teaspoon vanilla extract
1 teaspoon ground cinnamon
½ teaspoon ground nutmeg
½ teaspoon ground ginger
1 can (15 ounces [425 g]) pumpkin puree (not pumpkin pie mix)
½ cup (120 ml) water or apple juice

1. Wash the apples, then halve, core, peel, and dice them.
2. Transfer the apples to the slow cooker. Add the vanilla, cinnamon, nutmeg, and ginger. Stir to combine.
3. Add the pumpkin puree and the water or juice (or a combination of both) and stir.
4. Cover and cook on low for 6 to 8 hours for the best fusion of flavors and a saucy texture. Alternately, cook on high for 4 to 5 hours. Let the sauce cool in the slow cooker.

Preparation and Storage for Baby

When cooled, puree the sauce in batches. Use a handheld mixer or immersion blender and mix right in the slow cooker, or use a food processor to achieve a smoother texture. For babies, use water, formula, or breast milk as you continue to puree. You can also mash or partially puree the sauce and try to get some lumps, but this recipe will simmer down to a fairly smooth texture.

Store in the refrigerator for up to 3 days for babies.

To freeze, follow the stage two directions in "Freezing Homemade Baby Food" on page 28.

For the Family

This makes a great sauce for roasting chicken or pork and, of course, for spreading on biscuits and pancakes. Or try mixing it into cereal, oatmeal, or yogurt or spooning it warm over ice cream. Yes—ice cream!

❄ Freezes well, but you will probably see some ice crystals due to the high water content; mix to recombine.
● Vitamins A, B_6, C, and E, fiber, iron, potassium, and calcium

Triple Berry Sauce

The berries in this recipe are incredibly good for your health. Blueberries, in particular, are considered a superfood because of their high antioxidant, phytoflavinoid, and vitamin C and K content. My kids were always confused how blueberries could be a superfood when they were just little fruits; the size of something is not an accurate reflection of its power.

Age and Stage: 6 to 8 months+ | Stage One to Two | Second Foods and Beyond
Slow Cooker Size: 4 to 6 quarts (3.8 to 5.7 l); round

2 pints (500 g) fresh raspberries
1 bag (12 ounces [340 g]) fresh cranberries
2 pints (580 g) fresh blueberries
or
2 bags (1 pound [455 g] each) frozen mixed berries
3 medium apples, such as McIntosh
1 teaspoon vanilla extract
½ cup (120 ml) water or apple juice

1. If using fresh berries, wash and carefully pick through them and remove any stems or debris. Wash the apples, then halve, core, peel, and dice them.
2. Transfer the apples to the slow cooker. Top with the fresh or frozen berries. Add the vanilla and stir. Add the water or juice (or a combination of both) and stir to combine.
3. Cover and cook on low for 6 hours to produce the best fusion of flavors and a saucy texture. Alternately, cook on high for 4 to 5 hours. The cranberries will remain a bit firm. Let the sauce cool in the slow cooker.

Preparation and Storage for Baby

When cooled, puree the sauce in batches. Use a handheld mixer or immersion blender and mix right in the slow cooker, or use a food processor to achieve a smoother texture. For babies, use water, formula, or breast milk as you continue to puree. You can also mash or partially puree the sauce and try to get some lumps.

Store in the refrigerator for up to 3 days for babies.

To freeze, follow the stage two directions in "Freezing Homemade Baby Food" on page 28.

For the Family

Spread on biscuits or pancakes or mix into cereal, oatmeal, or yogurt. Or spoon warm over ice cream or blend into smoothies. Yes, I said ice cream again!

❄ Freezes well, but you will probably see some ice crystals due to the high water content of the apples and blueberries; mix to recombine. 🍎 Vitamins A, B_6, C, and E, fiber, iron, potassium, and calcium

Blueberry Peary Sauce

My kids always enjoyed dices of pears mixed with squished blueberries, plopped in a bowl or on their high chair trays. When you combine the fruits and slow-cook them, you get a tasty sauce that's great for drizzling over the dices and smooshes.

Age and Stage: 6 to 8 months+ | Stage One to Two | Second Foods and Beyond
Slow Cooker Size: 4 to 6 quarts (3.8 to 5.7 l); round

3 pints (870 g) fresh blueberries or 2 bags (1 pound [455 g] each) frozen blueberries
10 pears
1 teaspoon vanilla extract
½ teaspoon ground cinnamon
½ cup (120 ml) water or apple juice

1. If using fresh berries, wash and carefully pick through them and remove any stems or debris. Wash the pears, then halve, core, peel, and dice them.
2. Place the fresh or frozen blueberries in the slow cooker. Top with the pears. Add the vanilla and cinnamon and stir. Add the water or juice (or a combination of both) and stir to combine.
3. Cover and cook on low for 6 hours to produce the best fusion of flavors and a saucy texture. Alternately, cook on high for 4 to 5 hours. Let the sauce cool in the slow cooker.

Preparation and Storage for Baby

When cooled, puree the sauce in batches. Use a handheld mixer or immersion blender and mix right in the slow cooker, or use a food processor to achieve a smoother texture. For babies, use water, formula, or breast milk as you continue to puree. You can also mash or partially puree the sauce and try to get some lumps, but this recipe will simmer down to a fairly smooth texture.

Store in the refrigerator for up to 3 days for babies.

To freeze, follow the stage two directions in "Freezing Homemade Baby Food" on page 28.

For the Family

This sauce is delicious in smoothies and yummy when spread on biscuits or pancakes or mixed into cereal, oatmeal, or yogurt. Or spoon it warm over ice cream. Yes, I said ice cream for the third time!

❄ Freezes well, but you will probably see some ice crystals due to the high water content of the pears and blueberries; mix to recombine. 🍎 Vitamins A, B$_6$, C, and E, fiber, iron, potassium, and calcium

Cranberry Applesauce Sauce

Making cranberry applesauce is a great way to introduce your kids to the taste of cranberries. The applesauce gives the cranberries a natural sweetness that helps to cut the tartness.

Age and Stage: 6 to 8 months+ | Stage One to Two | Second Foods and Beyond
Slow Cooker Size: 4 to 6 quarts (3.8 to 5.7 l); round

> 2 bags (12 ounces [340 g] each) fresh or frozen cranberries (about 6 cups)
> 10 apples, such as Gala
> 1 teaspoon vanilla extract
> ½ teaspoon ground cinnamon
> ½ cup (120 ml) water or apple juice

1. Wash the cranberries and carefully pick through them and remove any stems or debris. Wash the apples, then halve, core, peel, and dice them.
2. Place the cranberries in the slow cooker. Top with the apples. Add the vanilla and cinnamon and stir. Add the water or juice (or a combination of both) and stir to combine.
3. Cover and cook on low for 5 to 6 hours to produce the best fusion of flavors and a saucy texture. Alternately, cook on high for 3 to 4 hours. The cranberries will remain a bit firm. Let the sauce cool in the slow cooker.

Preparation and Storage for Baby

When cooled, puree the sauce in batches. Use a handheld mixer or immersion blender and mix right in the slow cooker, or use a food processor to achieve a smoother texture. For babies, use water, formula, or breast milk as you continue to puree. You can also mash or partially puree the sauce and try to get some lumps, but this recipe will simmer down to a fairly smooth texture.

Store in the refrigerator for up to 3 days for babies.

To freeze, follow the stage two directions in "Freezing Homemade Baby Food" on page 28.

For the Family

This makes a great side with a traditional roasted turkey dinner, but it's also fabulous on turkey sandwiches and mixed into turkey or chicken salad. Did I say ice cream for this one? No, because I haven't tried it—yet!

❊ Freezes well, but you will probably see some ice crystals due to the high water content of the apples and cranberries; mix to recombine. 🍎 Vitamins A, B$_6$, C, and E, fiber, iron, potassium, and calcium

Figgy Pear Sauce

Figs are so, figgy. When you combine them with pears, the resulting sauce is less sticky and thick than it would be if you left the figs on their own.

Age and Stage: 6 to 8 months+ | Stage One to Two | Second Foods and Beyond
Slow Cooker Size: 4 to 6 quarts (3.8 to 5.7 l); round

15 dried mission figs (purple/black in color), unsulfured
7 pears
¼ teaspoon vanilla extract
½ teaspoon dried nutmeg
1 cup (235 ml) water or apple juice or ½ cup (120 ml) water and ½ cup (120 ml) apple cider

1. Wash the figs (if purchased from a bulk bin) and the pears. Cut the figs in halves or quarters. Halve, core, peel, and dice the pears.
2. Transfer the figs and pears to the slow cooker. Add the vanilla and nutmeg and stir. Add the water or juice (or water and cider) and stir to combine.
3. Cover and cook on low for 5 to 6 hours. Let the sauce cool in the slow cooker.

Preparation and Storage for Baby

When cooled, puree the sauce in batches. Use a handheld mixer or immersion blender and mix right in the slow cooker or use a food processor to achieve a smoother texture. For babies, use water, formula, or breast milk as you continue to puree.

Store in the refrigerator for up to 3 days for babies.

To freeze, follow the stage two directions in "Freezing Homemade Baby Food" on page 28.

For the Family

This makes a great sauce for roasted chicken or pork and, of course, for spreading on biscuits or pancakes or mixing into cereal, oatmeal, or yogurt. Or spoon it warm over ice cream. Yes, I said ice cream again. Do you notice a theme with these applesauces?

❄ Freezes well, but the figs may lend a sticky/tacky texture to the mix when you freeze it. You might see some ice crystals due to the high water content of the fruits; mix to recombine. 🍎 Vitamins A, B$_6$, C, and E, fiber, iron, potassium, and calcium

Peaches and Pears Sauce

Get extra peaches and pears so that you can chop and dice for finger foods for your baby.

Age and Stage: 6 to 8 months+ | Stage One to Two | Second Foods and Beyond
Slow Cooker Size: 4 to 6 quarts (3.8 to 5.7 l); round

10 fresh peaches or 1 bag (1 pound [455 g]) frozen peaches
10 pears
¼ teaspoon vanilla extract
½ cup (120 ml) water or apple juice or ¼ cup (60 ml) water and ¼ cup (60 ml) apple cider

1. Wash the peaches (if using fresh) and pears. Halve, pit, and peel the peaches. If large, cut into quarters. Halve, core, peel, and dice the pears.
2. Transfer the fresh or frozen peaches and the pears to the slow cooker. Add the vanilla and stir. Add the water or juice (or water and cider) and stir to combine.
3. Cover and cook on low for 5 to 6 hours. Let the sauce cool in the slow cooker.

Preparation and Storage for Baby

When cooled, puree the sauce in batches. Use a handheld mixer or immersion blender and mix right in the slow cooker, or use a food processor to achieve a smoother texture. For babies, use water, formula, or breast milk as you continue to puree.

Store in the refrigerator for up to 3 days for babies.

To freeze, follow the stage two directions in "Freezing Homemade Baby Food" on page 28.

For the Family

This is another great sauce for roasted chicken or pork. You can also spread it on biscuits or pancakes, mix it into cereal, oatmeal, rice pudding, or yogurt, or add it to your favorite smoothie.

❄ Freezes well, but you will probably see some ice crystals due to the high water content of the fruits; mix to recombine.　🍎 Vitamins A, B, C, and E, fiber, iron, potassium, and calcium

Peaches and Apples Sauce

When your kiddo asks you for some "pee-pples," you'll know she wants some of the delicious peach and apple puree you just made.

Age and Stage: 6 to 8 months+ | Stage One to Two | Second Foods and Beyond

Slow Cooker Size: 4 to 6 quarts (3.8 to 5.7 l); round

10 fresh peaches or 1 bag (1 pound [455 g]) frozen peaches

6 large apples, such as Gala

¼ teaspoon ground cinnamon

½ cup (120 ml) water or apple juice or ¼ cup (60 ml) water and ¼ cup (60 ml) apple cider

1. Wash the peaches (if using fresh) and apples. Halve, pit, and peel the peaches. If large, cut into quarters. Halve, core, peel, and dice the apples.
2. Transfer the fresh or frozen peaches and the apples to the slow cooker. Add the vanilla and stir. Add the water or juice (or water and cider) and stir to combine.
3. Cover and cook on low for 5 to 6 hours. Let the sauce cool in the slow cooker.

Preparation and Storage for Baby

When cool, puree the sauce in batches. Use a handheld mixer or immersion blender and mix right in the slow cooker, or use a food processor to achieve a smoother texture. For babies, use water, formula, or breast milk as you continue to puree.

Store in the refrigerator for up to 3 days for babies.

To freeze, follow the stage two directions in "Freezing Homemade Baby Food" on page 28.

For the Family

This is yet another great sauce for roasted chicken or pork, but if you add it into meatloaf (meatcake, as I tell my kids), you'll be amazed at the flavor. You can also spread it on biscuits or pancakes or mix it into cereal, oatmeal, rice pudding, or yogurt. Or add it to your favorite smoothie, use as a syrup for French toast, or spread on bagels. No, I haven't said ice cream, but by now, you know what to do!

❄ Freezes well, but you will probably see some ice crystals due to the high water content of the fruits; mix to recombine.

🍎 Vitamins A, B, C, and E, fiber, iron, potassium, and calcium

Peachy Pumpkin Sauce

So how much orange goodness can you even stand? Make this recipe and watch your littles smack their lips and then you'll have the answer.

Age and Stage: 6 to 8 months+ | Stage One to Two | Second Foods and Beyond
Slow Cooker Size: 4 to 6 quarts (3.8 to 5.7 l); oval

> 1 sugar pumpkin (5 to 6 pounds [2.3 to 2.7 kg]) or 2 cans (15 ounces [425 g] each) pumpkin puree (not the pumpkin pie mix)
> 10 fresh peaches or 1 bag (1 pound [455 g]) frozen peaches
> 1 teaspoon vanilla extract
> ½ cup (120 ml) water or apple juice or ¼ cup (60 ml) water and ¼ cup (60 ml) apple cider

1. If using fresh, wash the pumpkin and peaches. Cut the pumpkin in half and scoop out the seeds (save them to roast). Peel and dice each half. Halve, pit, and peel the peaches. If large, cut into quarters.
2. Transfer the diced pumpkin or pumpkin puree to the slow cooker. Add the fresh or frozen peaches and the vanilla. Stir to combine. Add the water or juice (or water and cider) and stir.
3. Cover and cook on low for 5 to 6 hours. The pumpkin will require a longer cooking time than the peaches will, so you may want to remove the peaches when they're soft and let the pumpkin continue to cook for 1 to 2 hours. Let the sauce cool in the slow cooker.

Preparation and Storage for Baby

When cool, puree the sauce in batches. Use a handheld mixer or immersion blender and mix right in the slow cooker, or use a food processor to achieve a smoother texture. For babies, use water, formula, or breast milk as you continue to puree.

Store in the refrigerator for up to 3 days for babies.

To freeze, follow the stage two directions in "Freezing Homemade Baby Food" on page 28.

For the Family

This is yet another great sauce for roasted chicken or pork, but if you add it into meatloaf (meatcake, as I tell my kids), you'll be amazed at the flavor. You can also spread it on biscuits or pancakes or mix it into cereal, oatmeal, rice pudding, or yogurt. Or add it to your favorite smoothie, use as a syrup for French toast, or spread on bagels. Or, of course, there's always ice cream . . . !

❄ Freezes well, but you will probably see some ice crystals due to the high water content of the fruits; mix to recombine. 🍎 Vitamins A, B, C, and E, fiber, iron, potassium, and calcium

Pumpkin Butter

This recipe for pumpkin butter is one that my family loves. It may not be the best option for babies under a certain age because I am including brown sugar and maple syrup. You can omit these if you'd like.

Age and Stage: 6 to 8 months+ | Stage One to Two | Second Foods and Beyond
Slow Cooker Size: 4 to 6 quarts (3.8 to 5.7 l); oval

2 sugar pumpkins (5 to 6 pounds each [2.3 to 2.7 kg]) or 3 cans (15 ounces [425 g] each) pumpkin puree (not the pumpkin pie mix)
2 teaspoons vanilla extract
2 teaspoons ground cinnamon
½ teaspoon ground nutmeg
½ teaspoon ground cloves
½ teaspoon ground ginger
½ cup (120 ml) apple cider
½ cup (115 g) packed brown sugar (optional)
¼ cup (80 g) maple syrup or ¼ cup (60 ml) water

1. If using fresh, wash the pumpkin. Cut it in half and scoop out the seeds (save them to roast). Peel and dice each half.
2. Transfer the fresh or canned pumpkin to the slow cooker. Add the vanilla, cinnamon, nutmeg, cloves, ginger, cider, brown sugar (if using), and maple syrup or water. Stir to combine.
3. Cover and cook on low for 5 to 6 hours. Let the sauce cool in the slow cooker.

Preparation and Storage for Baby

When cool, puree the sauce in batches. Use a handheld mixer or immersion blender and mix right in the slow cooker, or use a food processor to achieve a smoother texture. For babies, use water, formula, or breast milk as you continue to puree.

Store in the refrigerator for up to 3 days for babies.

To freeze, follow the stage two directions in "Freezing Homemade Baby Food" on page 28.

For the Family

This recipe is one that you will want to add to everything that you eat!

❄ Freezes well, but you will probably see some ice crystals due to the high water content of the pureed pumpkin; mix to recombine. 🍎 Vitamins A, B, C, and E, fiber, iron, potassium, and calcium

Raspberry Pear Sauce

Red pears—nothing more needs to be said. Present this dish to your kids and watch them light up when they see the color.

Age and Stage: 6 to 8 months+ | Stage One to Two | Second Foods and Beyond
Slow Cooker Size: 4 to 6 quarts (3.8 to 5.7 l); round

12 fresh pears, such as Anjou or red
3 pints (750 g) fresh raspberries or 1 bag (1 pound [455 g]) frozen raspberries
¼ teaspoon vanilla extract
½ cup (120 ml) water

1. Wash the pears and raspberries, if using fresh. Halve, core, peel, and dice the pears. Remove any leaves and stems from the raspberries.
2. Transfer the pears and fresh or frozen raspberries to the slow cooker. Add the vanilla and water and stir.
3. Cover and cook on low for 5 to 6 hours. Let the sauce cool in the slow cooker.

Preparation and Storage for Baby

When cool, puree the sauce in batches. Use a handheld mixer or immersion blender and mix right in the slow cooker, or use a food processor to achieve a smoother texture. For babies, use water, formula, or breast milk as you continue to puree.

You may want to push the sauce through a sieve to remove any remaining seeds when you're finished pureeing; the raspberry seeds may not puree well.

Store in the refrigerator for up to 3 days for babies.

To freeze, follow the stage two directions in "Freezing Homemade Baby Food" on page 28.

For the Family

This is another great sauce for roasted chicken or pork. Or spread it on biscuits or pancakes, mix it into cereal, oatmeal, rice pudding, or yogurt. You could also add it to your favorite smoothie.

❋ Freezes well, but you will probably see some ice crystals due to the high water content of the fruits (especially the raspberries); mix to recombine.   🍎 B vitamins as well as A, C, and E, plus iron, folate, calcium, magnesium, fiber, and protein   ★ Raspberries are known be allergenic for some people. If you or anyone in your family has a history of food allergies, contact your pediatrician about offering your baby foods that may be allergenic.

Peachy Raspberry Sauce

This recipe is just so yummy that your baby may try to stuff some into her pants to take with her.

Age and Stage: 6 to 8 months+ | Stage One to Two | Second Foods and Beyond
Slow Cooker Size: 4 to 6 quarts (3.8 to 5.7 l); round

10 fresh peaches or 1 bag (1 pound [455 g]) frozen peaches
3 pints (750 g) fresh raspberries or 1 bag (1 pound [455 g]) frozen raspberries
¼ teaspoon vanilla extract
½ cup (120 ml) water

1. If using fresh, wash the peaches and raspberries. Halve, pit, peel, and dice the peaches. Remove any leaves and stems from the raspberries.
2. Transfer the fresh or frozen peaches and raspberries to the slow cooker. Add the vanilla and water and stir.
3. Cover and cook on low for 5 to 6 hours. Let the sauce cool in the slow cooker.

Preparation and Storage for Baby

When cool, puree the sauce in batches. Use a handheld mixer or immersion blender and mix right in the slow cooker, or use a food processor to achieve a smoother texture. For babies, use water, formula, or breast milk as you continue to puree.

You may want to push the sauce through a sieve to remove any remaining seeds when you're finished pureeing; the raspberry seeds may not puree well.

Store in the refrigerator for up to 3 days for babies.

To freeze, follow the stage two directions in "Freezing Homemade Baby Food" on page 28.

For the Family

Yes, ice cream. There really is no need to say more, but here it is: you could also spread the sauce on biscuits or pancakes or mix it into cereal, oatmeal, rice pudding, yogurt, or your favorite smoothie.

❄ Freezes well, but you will probably see some ice crystals due to the high water content of the fruits (especially the raspberries); mix to recombine.　🍎 Vitamins A, B, C, and E, fiber, iron, potassium, and calcium
★ Raspberries are known be allergenic for some people. If you or anyone in your family has a history of food allergies, contact your pediatrician about offering your baby foods that may be allergenic.

Double Berry Applesauce

Applesauce is so simple to make that there are times when we should get all fancy and add other fruits to it. The nice thing about making a fancy applesauce is that your little one will be exposed a to flavorful combination that helps expand her palate.

Age and Stage: 6 to 8 months+ | Stage One to Two | Second Foods and Beyond
Slow Cooker Size: 4 to 6 quarts (3.8 to 5.7 l); round

> 3 pints (870 g) fresh strawberries or 1 bag (1 pound [455 g]) frozen strawberries
> 2 pints (580 g) fresh blueberries or 1 bag (1 pound [455 g]) frozen blueberries
> 8 large apples, such as McIntosh
> ½ teaspoon vanilla extract
> ½ cup (120 ml) water

1. If using fresh, wash the strawberries, blueberries, and apples. Remove any leaves and stems from the strawberries and blueberries. Halve, core, peel, and dice the apples.
2. Transfer the fresh or frozen fruit to the slow cooker. Add the vanilla and water and stir.
3. Cover and cook on low for 5 to 6 hours. Let the sauce cool in the slow cooker.

Preparation and Storage for Baby

When cool, puree the sauce in batches. Use a handheld mixer or immersion blender and mix right in the slow cooker, or use a food processor to achieve a smoother texture. For babies, use water, formula, or breast milk as you continue to puree.

You may want to push the sauce through a sieve to remove any remaining seeds when you're finished pureeing; the strawberry seeds may not puree well.

Store in the refrigerator for up to 3 days for babies.

To freeze, follow the stage two directions in "Freezing Homemade Baby Food" on page 28.

For the Family

Spread the sauce on biscuits or pancakes or mix it into cereal, oatmeal, rice pudding, yogurt, or your favorite smoothie. You can also mix this into your favorite barbecue sauce and brush on ribs or chicken that you will be smoking or grilling.

❄ Freezes well, but you will probably see some ice crystals due to the high water content of the fruits; mix to recombine. 🍎 Vitamins A, B, C, and E, fiber, iron, potassium, and calcium ★ Strawberries are known be allergenic for some people. If you or anyone in your family has a history of food allergies, contact your pediatrician about offering your baby foods that may be allergenic.

Vanilla Pears with Cinnamon

This recipe is included because it has amazing flavor and is very easy to make. Vanilla pears are great with anything, even chicken!

Age and Stage: 6 to 8 months+ | Stage One to Two | Second Foods and Beyond
Slow Cooker Size: 4 to 6 quarts (3.8 to 5.7 l); oval

10 pears, such as Anjou
½ teaspoon vanilla extract
½ teaspoon ground cinnamon
¼ cup (60 ml) water or apple juice

1. Wash the pears and then halve, core, and peel them.
2. Transfer the pear halves to the slow cooker. Add the vanilla and cinnamon and stir. Pour in the water or juice and stir to combine.
3. Cover and cook on low for 4 to 5 hours. Remove the pear halves to a bowl to cool.

Preparation and Storage for Baby

When the pear halves have cooled, you can puree them, mash them, or just leave them as they are.

To puree, use a handheld mixer or immersion blender, or use a food processor to achieve a smoother texture. The pears will likely puree to a smooth texture on their own, but if necessary, you can use water, formula, or breast milk as you continue to puree to thin the pears down.

Store in the refrigerator for up to 3 days for babies.

To freeze, follow the stage two directions in "Freezing Homemade Baby Food" on page 28.

For the Family

Serve the pear halves on plates and top each serving with half a scoop of ice cream (I know, I said it again!) and/or whipped cream for a tasty and mostly healthy dessert.

✳ Freezes well when pureed, but you will probably see some ice crystals due to the high water content of the pears; mix to recombine. 🍎 Vitamins A, B, C, and E, fiber, some iron, potassium, and calcium

8

Twenty Grain-Based Cereals for Any Time of Day

The cereal recipes in this chapter take traditional favorites and shake them up a bit. As your baby moves into toddlerhood and then into school age, you will find yourself adapting certain comfort and "stick to your belly" recipes to ever-changing tastes. Most of the following recipes will be suitable for babies who are 8 months of age and older. It is up to you as the parent to determine if your younger baby can enjoy these recipes. When in doubt, ask your baby's pediatrician.

Rinsing and Toasting Grains

Rinsing and/or toasting grains prior to cooking them can boost their flavor and make the grains easier to cook. Doing this is not required, but many cooks swear by thoroughly rinsing and toasting grains prior to preparing them. Here is a simple how-to for rinsing and toasting.

Rinsing grains: Add the grains to a fine-mesh strainer and rinse with cool water until the water runs clear. If you see bubbles (saponins) coming up from the grains as you rinse, continue to rinse until there are no more bubbles.

Toasting grains: Heat a skillet over medium-high heat and add the desired amount and type of grains. Stir the grains continuously. They will change to a darker color, and you'll smell an almost nutty aroma. Grains can also be toasted in the oven. Spread a thin layer of grains on a baking sheet and toast in a 350°F (180°C) oven for 10 to 15 minutes. The grains will turn dark and will smell a bit nutty. Toasting grains makes them cook faster.

The following grains are best when rinsed or toasted prior to cooking:

Quinoa (not a grain but actually a seed): Quinoa contains saponins, which tend to give off a bitter taste. Most quinoa is prerinsed, but consider rinsing anyway. You can also toast quinoa in a skillet or in the oven.

Millet: Toast millet for the best flavor and faster cooking.

Barley: Toast barley to bring out its flavor and to hurry cooking.

Kamut: This grain does not need to be toasted, but toasting it brings out a great crunchy texture.

Buckwheat/kasha: Buckwheat should be rinsed before you cook with it. Kasha, which is often used interchangeably with the word *buckwheat,* is actually buckwheat that has been roasted.

Cooking Single Grains in a Slow Cooker

The following are the typical grain-to-liquid ratios used for cooking common grains:

Steel-cut oats: 1 cup (135 g) steel-cut oats to 4 to 5 cups (945 ml to 1.2 l) liquid

Buckwheat: 1 cup groats (120 g) to 1½ cups (355 ml) water; it you want mushier buckwheat, use 2 cups (475 ml) water

Rice: 1 cup (195 g) rice to 2 cups (475 ml) liquid

Millet: 1 cup (220 g) millet to 3 cups (710 ml) water (for creamy consistency)

Kamut: 1 cup (184 g) kamut (berries) to 3 cups (710 ml) liquid

Quinoa: 1 cup (173 g) quinoa to 1½ cups (355 ml) liquid

Cornmeal: 1 cup (140 g) course cornmeal to 4 cups (945 ml) liquid; for polenta, use a 1 to 5 ratio to ensure creaminess

Once you've determined your grain-to-liquid ratio, cooking grains in a slow cooker is a simple three-step process:

1. Wipe the inside of the slow cooker vessel with butter.
2. Add the grain, liquid, and any other ingredients to the slow cooker. Stir to combine.
3. Cook on high for 2 to 3 hours or on low for 6 to 8 hours.

Velvety Vanilla Brown Rice

Rice is seldom thought of as a breakfast food, but when you make any type of sweet, as opposed to savory, rice dish, it can be served at breakfast.

Age and Stage: 8 months+ | Stage Two | Second Foods and Beyond
Slow Cooker Size: 6 quarts (5.7 l); oval

3 cups (570 g) brown rice
5 cups (1.2 l) water
1 cup (235 ml) low-fat milk
½ cup (115 g) whole milk yogurt
2 teaspoons vanilla extract

1. Rinse and drain the rice.
2. Wipe the inside of the slow cooker vessel with butter. Add the rice, water, milk, yogurt, and vanilla. Stir to combine.
3. Cover and cook on low for 6 to 7 hours. This can be cooked overnight, but it's best to cook it during the day so you can keep an eye on the cooking progress.

Preparation and Storage for Baby

Spoon out a few portions for baby, stir in any of the sauces you made from earlier recipes in this book, and allow to cool. You can puree the brown rice; however, you may not get a smooth result.

Store leftovers in the refrigerator for up to 3 days for babies, up to 5 days for adults.

To freeze, follow the stage two directions in "Freezing Homemade Baby Food" on page 28.

For the Family

This recipe yields a lazy brown rice pudding. Once you have taken portions out for baby, you can add more yogurt or milk and simmer for an hour longer; add raisins, chopped apples or bananas, and maple syrup or brown sugar.

✽ Freezes well, but some separation may occur when thawed; mix to combine.
🍎 B vitamins, iron, calcium, protein, and a large amount of magnesium and fiber

Overnight Apple Oatmeal

This is a favorite recipe for the winter months. No one likes getting up when it's dark and cold, but wake up to this warm and delicious oatmeal and everyone will be smiling. Offer your baby his own bowl and let him use his fingers or practice his spoon skills.

Age and Stage: 8 months+ | Stage Two | Second Foods and Beyond
Slow Cooker Size: 4 to 6 quarts (3.8 to 5.7 l); oval

5 apples, such as Granny Smith
1½ cups (203 g) steel-cut oats
7 cups (1.7 l) water or 4 cups (945 ml) water and 3 cups (710 ml) cider or low-fat milk
1 tablespoon (7 g) ground cinnamon
1 teaspoon vanilla extract
½ teaspoon ground ginger

1. Wash the apples and then halve, core, and peel them.
2. Wipe the inside of the slow cooker vessel with butter. Add the apples, oats, liquid, cinnamon, vanilla, and ginger. Stir to combine.
3. Cover and cook on low for 8 hours or overnight. Wake up and enjoy!

Preparation and Storage for Baby

Spoon out a portion for baby and allow to cool.

Store leftovers in the refrigerator for up to 3 days for babies, up to 5 days for adults.

To freeze, follow the stage two directions in "Freezing Homemade Baby Food" on page 28.

For the Family

Making warm cereals in the slow cooker overnight is a great way to get the whole family to show up at the breakfast table. Gather everyone and serve on the weekend or before school.

❄ Freezes well, but some separation may occur when thawed; mix to recombine.
🍎 B vitamins, including folate, as well as A, C, and E, plus fiber and iron, calcium, and magnesium

Overnight Buckwheat Cereal with Cinnamon Pears

Have your kids help you to freeze leftovers by using the plop method. Lay wax paper on a baking sheet and plop the cereal in circles on top. Cover with plastic wrap and then freeze. Once the plops are frozen, remove them from the baking sheet and store in a freezer bag.

Age and Stage: 8 months+ | Stage Two | Second Foods and Beyond

Slow Cooker Size: 4 to 6 quarts (3.8 to 5.7 l); oval

1½ cups (180 g) buckwheat groats

5 pears, such as Anjou

5 cups (1.2 l) water or 2½ cups (595 ml) water and 2½ cups (595 ml) unsweetened apple juice

1 tablespoon (7 g) ground cinnamon

1. Rinse and drain the buckwheat. Wash, halve, core, and peel the pears.
2. Wipe the inside of the slow cooker vessel with butter. Add the buckwheat, pears, liquid, and cinnamon. Stir to combine.
3. Cover and cook on low for 8 hours or overnight.

Preparation and Storage for Baby

Spoon out a portion for baby and allow to cool.

Store leftovers in the refrigerator for up to 3 days for babies, up to 5 days for adults.

To freeze, follow the stage two directions in "Freezing Homemade Baby Food" on page 28.

For the Family

Gather the family and serve on the weekend or before school.

❄ Freezes well, but some separation may occur when thawed; mix to recombine.

🍎 B vitamins, including folate, as well as A, C, and E, plus iron, calcium, magnesium, and fiber

Buckwheat Cereal with Maple Apples

Buckwheat always makes me think of the old television show *The Little Rascals*. It also makes me think of the fall and the time that my twins were feeding fistfuls of the cereal to the dog. I can still hear their gleeful cackles! Each had a hand down beside his high chair, and the dog was positioned between them, enjoying a tasty breakfast, too.

Age and Stage: 8 months+ | Stage Two | Second Foods and Beyond

Slow Cooker Size: 4 to 6 quarts (3.8 to 5.7 l); oval

1½ cups (180 g) buckwheat groats

5 apples, such as Granny Smith

5 cups (1.2 l) water or 2½ cups (595 ml) water and 2½ cups (595 ml) unsweetened apple juice

1 container (6 ounces [175 g]) maple Greek yogurt

¼ cup (80 g) real maple syrup

1 teaspoon ground cinnamon

1 tablespoon (7 g) ground flaxseed

1. Rinse and drain the buckwheat. Wash, halve, core, and peel the apples.
2. Wipe the inside of the slow cooker vessel with butter. Add the buckwheat, apples, liquid, yogurt, maple syrup, cinnamon, and flaxseed. Stir to combine.
3. Cover and cook on low for 8 hours or overnight.

Preparation and Storage for Baby

Spoon out a portion for baby and allow to cool.

Store leftovers in the refrigerator for up to 3 days for babies, up to 5 days for adults.

To freeze, follow the stage two directions in "Freezing Homemade Baby Food" on page 28.

For the Family

Gather the family and serve on the weekend or before school. Garnish with small dices of apples and raisins and/or cranberries; top with walnuts or almonds, too.

❄ Freezes well, but some separation may occur when thawed; mix to recombine.

🍎 B vitamins, including folate, as well as A, C, and E, plus iron, calcium, magnesium, and fiber

Banana Spice Oatmeal

Have your kids help assemble the ingredients and use a fork to mash the bananas. Getting kids involved in the kitchen is one way to teach them the importance of healthy eating.

Age and Stage: 8 months+ | Stage Two | Second Foods and Beyond
Slow Cooker Size: 4 to 6 quarts (3.8 to 5.7 l); oval

1 cup (135 g) steel-cut oats
2 small ripe bananas, mashed or sliced
5 cups (1.2 l) water
1 cup (235 ml) low-fat milk
1 tablespoon (7 g) ground cinnamon
1 teaspoon vanilla extract
1 tablespoon (7 g) ground flaxseed

1. Wipe the inside of the slow cooker vessel with butter.
2. Add the oats, bananas, water, milk, cinnamon, vanilla, and flaxseed. Stir to combine.
3. Cover and cook on low for 8 hours or overnight. Wake up and enjoy!

Preparation and Storage for Baby

Spoon out a portion for baby and allow to cool. Making warm cereals in the slow cooker overnight is a great way to ensure everyone has a chance to eat a warm, filling breakfast.

Store leftovers in the refrigerator for up to 3 days for babies, up to 5 days for adults.

To freeze, follow the stage two directions in "Freezing Homemade Baby Food" on page 28.

For the Family

Wake up to this yummy and filling breakfast on the weekend or before school and add your favorite toppings.

❋ Freezes well, but some separation may occur when thawed; mix to re-combine.
● B vitamins, including folate, as well as A, C, and E, plus iron, calcium, magnesium, and fiber

Tropical Grains

This recipe uses coconut yogurt to give the cereal a tropical flair as well as a nice creamy texture.

Age and Stage: 8 months+ | Stage Two | Second Foods and Beyond

Slow Cooker Size: 4 to 6 quarts (3.8 to 5.7 l); oval

½ cup (95 g) brown rice

½ cup (110 g) millet

1 banana

½ cup (68 g) steel-cut oats

1 container (6 ounces [175 g]) coconut Greek yogurt

6 cups (1.4 l) water, or a combination of 3 cups (710 ml) water and 3 cups (710 ml) either apple juice or cider, a nut or rice milk, or low-fat milk

1 teaspoon vanilla extract

1 teaspoon ground cinnamon

1. Rinse and drain the rice and millet. Peel and mash the banana.
2. Wipe the inside of the slow cooker vessel with butter.
3. Add the oats, rice, millet, banana, yogurt, liquid, vanilla, and cinnamon. Stir to combine.
4. Cover and cook on low for 8 hours or overnight.

Preparation and Storage for Baby

Spoon out a portion for baby and allow to cool. Making warm cereals in the slow cooker overnight is a great way to get the whole family to show up at the breakfast table.

Store leftovers in the refrigerator for up to 3 days for babies, up to 5 days for adults.

To freeze, follow the stage two directions in "Freezing Homemade Baby Food" on page 28.

For the Family

For a real tropical treat, try using toppings such as coconut flakes, dried pineapple, mango, or a combination of the three.

❋ Freezes well, but some separation may occur when thawed; mix to recombine.

🍎 B vitamins, including folate, and A, C, and E, plus iron, calcium, magnesium, and fiber

Warm and Sassy Millet

Millet is for the birds—really. Your kids will get a kick out of the fact that you are serving them bird cereal.

Age and Stage: 8 months+ | Stage Two | Second Foods and Beyond
Slow Cooker Size: 6 quarts (5.7 l); oval

    3 cups (660 g) millet
    9 cups (2.1 l) water
    1 cup (235 ml) low-fat milk
    ½ cup (115 g) plain whole-milk yogurt
    2 teaspoons vanilla extract
    1 teaspoon ground cloves
    1 teaspoon ground nutmeg

1. Rinse and drain the millet. If desired, toast it in a dry skillet over medium-high heat until fragrant.
2. Wipe the inside of the slow cooker vessel with butter.
3. Add the millet, water, milk, yogurt, vanilla, cloves, and nutmeg. Stir to combine.
4. Cover and cook on low for 6 to 7 hours. This can be cooked overnight, but it's best to cook it during the day so you can keep an eye on the cooking progress. Millet will sometimes cook quite quickly.

Preparation and Storage for Baby

When cooked, spoon out a few portions for baby, stir in any of the sauces you made from earlier recipes in the book, and allow to cool. You can puree the millet; however, you may not get a smooth result.

Store leftovers in the refrigerator for up to 3 days for babies, up to 5 days for adults.

To freeze, follow the stage two directions in "Freezing Homemade Baby Food" on page 28.

For the Family

This recipe yields a fluffy but creamy millet cereal. Top with yogurt, raisins, chopped apples or bananas, nuts, and maple syrup or brown sugar.

❄ Freezes well, but some separation may occur when thawed; mix to recombine.
● Loaded with iron, calcium, protein, and a large amount of magnesium and fiber

Creamy Blueberry and Apple Oatmeal

This is another favorite oatmeal recipe that's great to serve your baby when she's practicing her spoon skills; the cereal will cling nicely.

Age and Stage: 8 months+ | Stage Two | Second Foods and Beyond
Slow Cooker Size: 4 to 6 quarts (3.8 to 5.7 l); oval

> 2 apples, such as Granny Smith
> 1½ cups (203 g) steel-cut oats
> 1 cup (155 g) frozen blueberries
> 7 cups (1.7 l) water or 4 cups (945 ml) water and 3 cups (710 ml) low-fat milk
> 1 tablespoon (7 g) ground cinnamon
> 1 teaspoon vanilla extract
> 1 tablespoon (7 g) ground flaxseed

1. Wash, halve, core, and peel the apples. Cut into chunks.
2. Wipe the inside of the slow cooker vessel with butter.
3. Add the oats, apples, blueberries, liquid, cinnamon, vanilla, and flaxseed. Stir to combine.
4. Cover and cook on low for 6 to 8 hours or overnight. Wake up and enjoy!

Preparation and Storage for Baby

Spoon out a portion for baby and allow to cool.

Store leftovers in the refrigerator for up to 3 days for babies, up to 5 days for adults.

To freeze, follow the stage two directions in "Freezing Homemade Baby Food" on page 28.

For the Family

Enjoy any time of the day!

❄ Freezes well, but some separation may occur when thawed; mix to recombine.
🍎 B vitamins, including folate, and A, C, and E, plus iron, calcium, magnesium, and fiber

Granola with Fruit and Cream

This is also known as the lazy cereal, and I don't hide the fact that it truly is. Sometimes, the simplest things make the best meals and dishes. The bonus here is that you can have your kids dump out the granola into the slow cooker.

Age and Stage: 8 months+ | Stage Two | Second Foods and Beyond

Slow Cooker Size: 4 to 6 quarts (3.8 to 5.7 l); oval

2 boxes or bags (12 ounces [340 g] each) granola (any type you prefer)

2 cups (475 ml) water

1 cup (235 ml) low-fat milk

1 tablespoon (7 g) ground cinnamon

1 teaspoon vanilla extract

1 tablespoon (7 g) ground flaxseed

1 cup (245 g) applesauce or pumpkin butter

1. Wipe the inside of the slow cooker vessel with butter.
2. Add the granola, water, milk, cinnamon, vanilla, flaxseed, and applesauce or pumpkin butter. Stir to combine.
3. Cover and cook on low for 6 to 8 hours or overnight. Wake up and enjoy!

Preparation and Storage for Baby

Spoon out a portion for baby and allow to cool.

Store leftovers in the refrigerator for up to 3 days for babies, up to 5 days for adults.

To freeze, follow the stage two directions in "Freezing Homemade Baby Food" on page 28.

For the Family

Enjoy any time of the day! Top with Greek yogurt and drizzle with maple syrup.

❄ Freezes well, but some separation may occur when thawed; mix to recombine.

🍎 B vitamins, including folate, and A, C, and E, plus iron, calcium, magnesium, and fiber

Kamut

This ancient grain is full of delicious nutrition, and it's fun to say, too. It is pronounced "kah-moot." Have fun with your little ones and try to make a few rhymes with kah-moot in them.

Age and Stage: 8 months+ | Stage Two | Second Foods and Beyond
Slow Cooker Size: 4 to 6 quarts (3.8 to 5.7 l); round

1 cup (172 g) kamut
3 cups (710 ml) water
1 tablespoon (7 g) ground cinnamon
1 teaspoon vanilla extract
1 tablespoon (7 g) ground flaxseed

1. Wipe the inside of the slow cooker vessel with butter.
2. Add the kamut, water, cinnamon, vanilla, and flaxseed. Stir to combine.
3. Cover and cook on low for 6 to 8 hours or overnight.

Preparation and Storage for Baby

Spoon out a portion for baby and allow to cool.

Store leftovers in the refrigerator for up to 3 days for babies, up to 5 days for adults.

To freeze, follow the stage two directions in "Freezing Homemade Baby Food" on page 28.

For the Family

Enjoy any time of the day! Top with your favorite toppings and drizzle with maple syrup.

❄ Freezes well, but some separation may occur when thawed; mix to recombine.
🍎 B vitamins, including folate, and iron, calcium, magnesium, phosphorus, protein, and fiber

Steel-Cut Oats and Kamut

When you just can't decide what type of cereal you should make, mix the grains up and create a new dish.

Age and Stage: 8 months+ | Stage Two | Second Foods and Beyond
Slow Cooker Size: 4 to 6 quarts (3.8 to 5.7 l); round

1 cup (135 g) steel-cut oats
1 cup (172 g) kamut
7 cups (1.7 l) water
1 teaspoon vanilla extract
1 teaspoon ground ginger
1 teaspoon ground nutmeg
1 tablespoon (7 g) ground flaxseed

1. Wipe the inside of the slow cooker vessel with butter.
2. Add the oats, kamut, water, vanilla, ginger, nutmeg, and flaxseed. Stir to combine.
3. Cover and cook on low for 6 to 8 hours or overnight.

Preparation and Storage for Baby

Spoon out a portion for baby and allow to cool.

Store leftovers in the refrigerator for up to 3 days for babies, up to 5 days for adults.

To freeze, follow the stage two directions in "Freezing Homemade Baby Food" on page 28.

For the Family

Enjoy any time of the day! Add your favorite toppings and drizzle with maple syrup.

❄ Freezes well, but some separation may occur when thawed; mix to recombine.
🍎 B vitamins, including folate, plus iron, calcium, magnesium, phosphorus, protein, and fiber

Maple Peaches and Cream Oatmeal

This cereal will cling nicely to a spoon, so it's another favorite oatmeal recipe for babies who are learning to scoop up food with a spoon instead of their fingers.

Age and Stage: 8 months+ | Stage Two | Second Foods and Beyond
Slow Cooker Size: 4 to 6 quarts (3.8 to 5.7 l); oval

1 cup (250 g) frozen peaches
1½ cups (203 g) steel-cut oats
7 cups (1.7 l) water or 4 cups (945 ml) water and 3 cups (710 ml) low-fat milk
½ cup (161 g) maple syrup
1 tablespoon (7 g) ground cinnamon
1 teaspoon vanilla extract
1 tablespoon (7 g) ground flaxseed

1. Wipe the inside of the slow cooker vessel with butter.
2. Add the peaches, oats, liquid, maple syrup, cinnamon, vanilla, and flaxseed. Stir to combine.
3. Cover and cook on low for 6 to 8 hours or overnight. Wake up and enjoy!

Preparation and Storage for Baby

Spoon out a portion for baby and allow to cool.

Store leftovers in the refrigerator for up to 3 days for babies, up to 5 days for adults.

To freeze, follow the stage two directions in "Freezing Homemade Baby Food" on page 28.

For the Family

Enjoy any time of the day!

❄ Freezes well, but some separation may occur when thawed; mix to recombine.
🍎 B vitamins, including folate, plus A, C, and E, as well as iron, calcium, magnesium, and fiber

Quinoa Oatmeal with Blueberries and Bananas

Yes, the recipe title is a bit long, but you and your kiddos are going to love this cereal anyway.

Age and Stage: 8 months+ | Stage Two | Second Foods and Beyond
Slow Cooker Size: 4 to 6 quarts (3.8 to 5.7 l); oval

1 cup (173 g) quinoa
2 small bananas
1 cup (80 g) oats
1 cup (155 g) frozen blueberries or 1 cup (220 g) blueberry sauce
9 cups (2.1 l) water
½ cup (161 g) maple syrup
1 teaspoon vanilla extract
1 tablespoon (7 g) ground flaxseed

1. Rinse and drain the quinoa. Peel and chop the bananas.
2. Wipe the inside of the slow cooker vessel with butter.
3. Add the quinoa, oats, bananas, blueberries or blueberry syrup, water, maple syrup, vanilla, and flaxseed. Stir to combine.
4. Cover and cook on low for 6 to 8 hours or overnight.

Preparation and Storage for Baby

Spoon out a portion for baby and allow to cool.

Store leftovers in the refrigerator for up to 3 days for babies, up to 5 days for adults.

To freeze, follow the stage two directions in "Freezing Homemade Baby Food" on page 28.

For the Family

Enjoy any time of the day!

❄ Freezes well, but some separation may occur when thawed; mix to recombine.
● B vitamins, including folate, plus A and C, iron, calcium, magnesium, fiber, and protein

Toasty Maple Quinoa with Apples

Here is another great word to play with. Have your kids say "keen-wah" and see if they find it as funny as my kids did when they were younger.

Age and Stage: 8 months+ | Stage Two | Second Foods and Beyond

Slow Cooker Size: 4 to 6 quarts (3.8 to 5.7 l); oval

2 apples, such as McIntosh
1 cup (173 g) quinoa
3 cups (710 ml) water
½ cup (161 g) maple syrup
1 tablespoon (7 g) ground cinnamon
1 teaspoon vanilla extract
1 tablespoon (7 g) ground flaxseed

1. Wash, halve, core, and peel the apples, then dice. Rinse and drain the quinoa.
2. Wipe the inside of the slow cooker vessel with butter.
3. Add the quinoa, apples, water, maple syrup, cinnamon, vanilla, and flaxseed. Stir to combine.
4. Cover and cook on low for 6 to 8 hours or overnight.

Preparation and Storage for Baby

Spoon out a portion for baby and allow to cool.

Store leftovers in the refrigerator for up to 3 days for babies, up to 5 days for adults.

To freeze, follow the stage two directions in "Freezing Homemade Baby Food" on page 28.

For the Family

Enjoy any time of the day!

❄ Freezes well, but some separation may occur when thawed; mix to recombine.
🍎 Folate, iron, calcium, magnesium, fiber, and protein

Maple Cinnamon Vanilla Quinoa Breakfast

Quinoa has a slightly nutty flavor, and the addition of maple syrup takes the taste to a higher level.

Age and Stage: 8 months+ | Stage Two | Second Foods and Beyond

Slow Cooker Size: 3 to 4 quarts (2.8 to 3.8 l); round

1 cup (173 g) quinoa

3 cups (710 ml) water

½ cup (161 g) maple syrup

1 teaspoon vanilla extract

1 teaspoon ground cinnamon

1 tablespoon (7 g) ground flaxseed

1. Rinse and drain the quinoa.
2. Wipe the inside of the slow cooker vessel with butter.
3. Add the quinoa, water, maple syrup, vanilla, cinnamon, and flaxseed. Stir to combine.
4. Cover and cook on low for 6 to 8 hours or overnight.

Preparation and Storage for Baby

Spoon out a portion for baby and allow to cool.

Store leftovers in the refrigerator for up to 3 days for babies, up to 5 days for adults.

To freeze, follow the stage two directions in "Freezing Homemade Baby Food" on page 28.

For the Family

Enjoy any time of the day!

❄ Freezes well, but some separation may occur when thawed; mix to recombine.

🍎 Folate, iron, calcium, magnesium, fiber, and protein

Warm Post Grape-Nuts and Cream

Yes, this is another "lazy cereal," but how many of us consistently have the time to put together a more complex mix for cereals? When you make this, you don't have to give away the secret.

Age and Stage: 8 months+ | Stage Two | Second Foods and Beyond

Slow Cooker Size: 4 to 6 quarts (3.8 to 5.7 l); oval

1 box (20.5 ounces [581 g]) Post Grape-Nuts cereal

4 cups (945 ml) water

2 cups (475 ml) low-fat milk

1 container (5.3 ounces [150 g]) Greek yogurt (plain, vanilla, or even a fruit flavor that the whole family enjoys)

1 teaspoon vanilla extract

½ teaspoon ground nutmeg

1. Wipe the inside of the slow cooker vessel with butter.
2. Add the cereal, water, milk, yogurt, vanilla, and nutmeg. Stir to combine.
3. Cover and cook on low for 6 to 8 hours or overnight.

Preparation and Storage for Baby

Spoon out a portion for baby and allow to cool.

Store leftovers in the refrigerator for up to 3 days for babies, up to 5 days for adults.

To freeze, follow the stage two directions in "Freezing Homemade Baby Food" on page 28.

For the Family

Enjoy any time of the day! Best when drizzled with maple syrup or sprinkled with brown sugar.

❄ Freezes well, but some separation may occur when thawed; mix to recombine.

● B vitamins, including folate, plus A, iron, calcium, magnesium, and fiber

Pumpkin Spice Breakfast Rice

Think of this dish as your new favorite autumn rice cereal. It's warm and filling and celebrates fall.

Age and Stage: 8 months+ | Stage Two | Second Foods and Beyond
Slow Cooker Size: 6 quarts (5.7 l); oval

1½ cups (293 g) jasmine rice
2 cups (475 ml) water
1 cup (235 ml) low-fat milk
½ cup (115 g) whole milk yogurt
½ cup (125 g) Spiced Apple Pumpkin Sauce (page 125)
2 teaspoons vanilla extract
1 teaspoon ground nutmeg
1 teaspoon ground cinnamon
1 teaspoon ground ginger

1. Rinse and drain the rice.
2. Wipe the inside of the slow cooker vessel with butter.
3. Add the rice, water, milk, yogurt, Spiced Apple Pumpkin Sauce, vanilla, nutmeg, cinnamon, and ginger. Stir to combine.
4. Cover and cook on low for 6 to 7 hours. This recipe can be cooked overnight, but it's best to cook it during the day so you can keep an eye on the cooking progress.

Preparation and Storage for Baby

Spoon out a few portions for baby, stir in any of the sauces you made from earlier recipes in the book, and allow to cool. You can puree the rice; however, you may not get a smooth texture.

Store leftovers in the refrigerator for up to 3 days for babies, up to 5 days for adults.

To freeze, follow the stage two directions in "Freezing Homemade Baby Food" on page 28.

For the Family

This recipe yields what I call a lazy rice pudding. Once you have taken portions out for baby, you could add more yogurt or milk and simmer for an hour longer; add raisins, chopped apples or bananas, and maple syrup or brown sugar.

❋ Freezes well, but some separation may occur when thawed; mix to recombine.
🍎 B vitamins, iron, calcium, protein, and a large amount of magnesium and fiber

Breakfast Rice Pudding

Rice pudding comes in all flavors and textures. This is a creamy breakfast "pudding" that also retains the texture of the rice. It's a great recipe for babies to practice their spoon skills or to just paint the high chair tray!

Age and Stage: 8 months+ | Stage Two | Second Foods and Beyond
Slow Cooker Size: 4 to 6 quarts (3.8 to 5.7 l); oval

1½ cups (293 g) Arborio (risotto-type) rice
5 cups (1.2 l) low-fat milk
½ cup (115 g) whole milk yogurt
2 teaspoons vanilla extract
1 teaspoon ground nutmeg
1 teaspoon ground cinnamon
½ teaspoon ground cloves

1. Rinse and drain the rice.
2. Wipe the inside of the slow cooker vessel with butter.
3. Add the rice, milk, yogurt, vanilla, nutmeg, cinnamon, and cloves. Stir to combine.
4. Cover and cook on low for 6 to 7 hours. This recipe can be cooked overnight, but it's best to cook it during the day so you can keep an eye on the cooking progress.

Preparation and Storage for Baby

Spoon out a few portions for baby, stir in any of the sauces you made from earlier recipes in the book, and allow to cool. You can puree the rice; however, you may not get a smooth texture.

Store leftovers in the refrigerator for up to 3 days for babies, up to 5 days for adults.

To freeze, follow the stage two directions in "Freezing Homemade Baby Food" on page 28.

For the Family

Once you have taken portions out for baby, fix yourself a bowl and top with yogurt, a drizzle of maple syrup, and sliced almonds and dried cranberries.

❄ Freezes well, but some separation may occur when thawed; mix to recombine.
🍎 B vitamins, iron, protein, and a large amount of selenium, magnesium, and fiber

Polenta Cornmeal Mush Mash

Polenta is cornmeal and cornmeal can be polenta. Grits can be polenta, too. As you can see, cornmeal can be prepared many different ways and is called many different names, depending on the region and ethnicity of the cook who prepares it. I always call this "cornmeal mush" for the kids. Just say, "Hey, let me put some mush in your bowl!" and enthusiastic nods erupt.

Age and Stage: 8 months+ | Stage Two | Second Foods and Beyond
Slow Cooker Size: 4 to 6 quarts (3.8 to 5.7 l); oval

2 cups (275 g) fine (not course) cornmeal polenta (do not use quick-cooking polenta)
3 cups (710 ml) milk
3 cups (710 ml) water
1 cup (120 g) grated cheese, such as cheddar, colby jack, or a Mexican blend
Butter
Ground pepper

1. Wipe the inside of the slow cooker vessel with butter.
2. Add the cornmeal, milk, and water. Stir to combine.
3. Cover and cook on high for 1 to 2 hours. Turn the slow cooker to low and cook, checking occasionally, for an additional 5 to 6 hours or until all of the liquid is absorbed. Add the cheese and stir until combined. Add butter and pepper to taste.

Preparation and Storage for Baby

Spoon out a few portions for baby and allow to cool. Instead of the cheese, butter, and pepper, you could add any of the sauces you made from earlier recipes in this book.

Store leftovers in the refrigerator for up to 3 days for babies, up to 5 days for adults.

To freeze, follow the stage two directions in "Freezing Homemade Baby Food" on page 28.

For the Family

This makes a large batch of polenta. You can make it savory by adding Italian seasonings plus garlic powder or minced garlic. To store it, you can spread the polenta mush on a buttered baking sheet or in a shallow baking dish and refrigerate. Once firm, cut in sections and then freeze portions for convenience.

❄ Freezes well, but some separation may occur when thawed; mix to recombine.
🍎 B vitamins, iron, calcium, protein, and a large amount of magnesium and fiber

Southern Grits

Buttered and cheesy, savory, or sweet, there are so many ways to prepare grits. Below, I offer three different cooking methods; choose the one that best matches your schedule for the day. Grits are almost the same as polenta but not quite.

Age and Stage: 8 months+ | Stage Two | Second Foods and Beyond
Slow Cooker Size: 4 to 6 quarts (3.8 to 5.7 l); oval

2 cups (328 g) grits (do not use quick-cooking grits)
6 cups (1.4 l) water
Butter
Ground pepper

METHOD 1

1. Wipe the inside of the slow cooker vessel with butter.
2. Add the grits and water. Stir or whisk to combine.
3. Cover and cook on low for 6 hours or until all of the liquid is absorbed. Add butter and pepper to taste.

METHOD 2

1. Wipe the inside of the slow cooker vessel with butter.
2. In a medium saucepan, bring the water to a boil. Add the grits. Boil for 3 minutes, whisking constantly. Transfer the grits to the slow cooker.
3. Cover and cook on high for 2 hours or until all of the liquid is absorbed. Add butter and pepper to taste.

METHOD 3

1. Wipe the inside of the slow cooker vessel with butter.
2. Add the grits and water. Stir or whisk to combine.
3. Cover and cook on high for 1 hour. Set the slow cooker on low and cook for 4 to 5 hours or until all of the liquid is absorbed. Add butter and pepper to taste.

Preparation and Storage for Baby

Spoon out a few portions for baby, stir in any of the sauces you made from earlier recipes in the book, and allow to cool.

Store leftovers in the refrigerator for up to 3 days for babies, up to 5 days for adults.

To freeze, follow the stage two directions in "Freezing Homemade Baby Food" on page 28.

For the Family

This makes a large batch of grits. Divide into portions for storage or store in 1 large container. Grits will not solidify as well as polenta.

❄ Freezes well, but some separation may occur when thawed; mix to recombine.
● B vitamins, iron, calcium, protein, and a large amount of magnesium and fiber

9

Third Foods:
Recipes for Fingers, Spoons, and Plates to Please Your Entire Family

The recipes that follow create meals that will please both your older (stage two or three) baby as well as your entire family. In the process, the recipes save you valuable time because there's no need to prepare something separate for baby.

Note that many of these recipes use meat, poultry, or fish. Just a reminder: It was once "the rule" that you should never place raw meat into a slow cooker and that the meat should always be seared and partially pan-cooked prior to going into the slow cooker. However, food safety experts now agree that as long as the meat is brought to its proper minimum safe temperature during the cooking process, it is completely safe to cook raw meats in the slow cooker.

The following are the appropriate safe temperatures to which proteins should be cooked:

- Beef: 160°F (70°C)
- Poultry: 165°F (75°C)
- Pork: 160°F (70°C)
- Fish: 145°F (65°C)

Most slow cookers will cook between 190°F and 300°F (90°C and 150°C). Therefore, as long as the food that you are cooking is brought to the proper temperature, there will be no food safety risks with slow-cooking meat, poultry, and fish.

If you have a little extra time and would like to brown or sear meat (for the golden brown color or to help sear in the juices) before placing it in the slow cooker, the process isn't difficult:

- Rinse the meat and pat dry with paper towels.
- Season with ground pepper and other seasonings of your choice, if desired.
- Heat some olive oil in a skillet.
- Place the meat in the skillet and cook or sear; be sure to turn the meat to get an even browning/sear on all sides.

Again, remember that this step is optional. And, of course, always wash your hands after handling raw meat, poultry, or fish.

A side note: You may notice that some of the seasoning measurements seem "small" for the size of the recipe. Because these meals will also be served to your little ones, the seasoning additions are mild. Please feel free to add more should you like a more flavorful dish and feel comfortable that your kiddos will enjoy more flavor, too. Of course, you could also remove the seasonings entirely if you prefer.

Lemon Chicken with Sweet Potatoes

Chicken and sweet potatoes is a classic combination that the majority of babies and toddlers love. When serving this to your baby or toddler, add a bit of butter to their portion for a nice flavor boost and an extra bit of healthy fat. My boys loved when I would add applesauce to their bowl of chicken and sweet potatoes.

Age and Stage: 8 months+ | Stage Two or Three | Second and Third Foods and Beyond
Slow Cooker Size: 6 quarts (5.7 l); oval

3 large sweet potatoes
1 whole chicken (5 to 6 pounds [2.3 to 2.7 kg])
1 lemon
Ground pepper
Dried rosemary
Dried sage
1 tablespoon (10 g) minced garlic

1. Wash, peel, and chop or dice the sweet potatoes.
2. Rinse the chicken and pat it dry with paper towels. Place on a cutting board. Wash the lemon and cut it in half. Stuff the lemon halves inside the cavity of the chicken. Sprinkle the pepper, rosemary, and sage over the chicken, to taste.
3. Transfer the chicken to the slow cooker. Add the sweet potatoes and garlic.
4. Cover and cook on low for 7 to 8 hours or on high for 4 to 5 hours or until a thermometer inserted in a breast registers 165°F (75°C) and the juices run clear.

Preparation and Storage for Baby

Remove the chicken and sweet potatoes from the slow cooker and set aside to cool. Mash or puree the sweet potatoes as needed to serve to your baby. Carve the chicken as desired and chop or puree a portion of the chicken to serve to baby.

Store leftovers in the refrigerator for up to 3 days for babies, up to 5 days for adults.

To freeze, follow the stage three directions in "Freezing Homemade Baby Food" on page 28.

For the Family

Prepare a side of wild rice or rice pilaf to accompany the chicken and sweet potatoes.

Chicken and lemon is a flavor combination that can't be beat! If you don't have any lemons, you could use 2 tablespoons (28 ml) of bottled lemon juice instead.

❄ Freezes well.   🍎 B vitamins, including folate, plus A, C, and E, iron, calcium, magnesium, fiber, and protein

Pork Tenderloin with Apples and Sweet Potatoes

As with the chicken and sweet potatoes recipe on the previous page, the addition of applesauce would make this combination one that's hard to resist. This time, we are adding the apples directly to the slow cooker to really infuse the flavors.

Age and Stage: 8 months+ | Stage Two or Three | Second and Third Foods and Beyond
Slow Cooker Size: 6 quarts (5.7 l); oval

3 medium sweet potatoes
4 large apples, such as McIntosh
1 pork tenderloin roast (5 to 6 pounds [2.3 to 2.7 kg])
1 teaspoon *each*: ground pepper, dried thyme, dried rosemary, and garlic powder
    (optional, for savory flavor)
1 teaspoon *each*: ground cinnamon and ground nutmeg, plus 2 tablespoons (40 g) maple syrup
    (optional, for a sweet flavor)
½ cup (120 ml) vegetable broth

1. Wash, peel, and chop or dice the sweet potatoes. Wash, halve, core, and peel the apples. Cut into thick slices.
2. Rinse the pork tenderloin and pat it dry with paper towels. If desired, sear the tenderloin in a hot skillet with a bit of olive oil.
3. Transfer the raw or seared pork tenderloin to the slow cooker. Sprinkle the herb/spice combination of your choice over the tenderloin. Add the sweet potatoes and apples to the slow cooker. If opting for the sweet flavor combination, drizzle with the maple syrup. Pour in the broth.
4. Cover and cook on low for 6 hours or on high for 4 hours or until a thermometer inserted in the center of the tenderloin registers 160°F (70°C) and the juices run clear.

Preparation and Storage for Baby

Remove the tenderloin, apples, and sweet potatoes from the slow cooker and set aside to cool. Mash or puree the sweet potatoes and apples as needed to serve to your baby. You could mash them together or separately. Slice the tenderloin as desired and chop or puree a portion of it to serve to baby.

Store leftovers in the refrigerator for up to 3 days for babies, up to 5 days for adults.

To freeze, follow the stage three directions in "Freezing Homemade Baby Food" on page 28.

For the Family

It's a meal!

Make this recipe savory or sweet; no matter which you choose, it will be a keeper!

❄ Freezes well, but some separation may occur when thawed; mix to recombine.
● B vitamins, including folate, plus A, C, and E, iron, calcium, magnesium, fiber, and protein

Lentils and Beef with Carrots

What a high-protein meal this recipe delivers, and it's tasty, too. Keep the lentils and carrots a bit on the al dente side so your little one can use a spoon or his fingers.

Age and Stage: 8 months+ | Stage Two or Three | Second and Third Foods and Beyond
Slow Cooker Size: 4 to 6 quarts (3.8 to 5.7 l); round

4 large carrots
1 cup (8 oz [225 g]) red or brown lentils
1 pound (455 g) stew beef, cubed
1 tablespoon (15 ml) olive oil
1 teaspoon ground pepper
1 teaspoon ground turmeric
1 teaspoon dried sage
1 teaspoon dried rosemary
1 tablespoon (10 g) minced garlic
2 cups (475 ml) water
1 cup (235 ml) beef broth

1. Wash, peel, and chop or dice the carrots into small pieces. Rinse and drain the lentils. Pick through them and discard any debris.
2. Rinse the beef and pat dry with paper towels. If desired, sear the beef cubes in a hot skillet with a bit of olive oil.
3. Grease the slow cooker with the olive oil. Transfer the raw or seared beef to the slow cooker. Add the carrots and lentils. Sprinkle the pepper, turmeric, sage, rosemary, and garlic over everything. Pour in the water and broth.
4. Cover and cook on low for 8 hours or on high for 4 to 5 hours or until the beef is no longer pink.

Preparation and Storage for Baby

Remove the beef, carrots, and lentils from the slow cooker and set aside to cool. Mash or puree the carrots as needed to serve to your baby. Mash a few of the beef cubes or chop or puree to serve to baby.

Store leftovers in the refrigerator for up to 3 days for babies, up to 5 days for adults.

To freeze, follow the stage three directions in "Freezing Homemade Baby Food" on page 28.

For the Family

It's a meal!

> *Lentils are full of protein, and when you add beef to a lentil dish, it's pure protein power.*

❄ Freezes well.   🍎 B vitamins, including folate, plus A, C, and E, iron, calcium, magnesium, fiber, and protein

Chicken with Apples and Beets

Chicken, beets, and apples are a tasty combination that should please all of the hungry people at your dinner table. Don't be alarmed by the purple hue that the chicken and apples may take on. Your kids will love it.

Age and Stage: 8 months+ | Stage Two or Three | Second and Third Foods and Beyond
Slow Cooker Size: 4 to 6 quarts (3.8 to 5.7 l); round

4 large beets
4 large apples, such as Granny Smith or McIntosh
6 boneless, skinless chicken breasts, trimmed of fat
1 teaspoon *each*: ground pepper, dried sage, dried rosemary, and garlic powder or fresh minced (optional, for savory flavor)
½ teaspoon *each*: ground cinnamon, ground nutmeg, and ground ginger (optional, for sweet flavor)
1 cup (235 ml) water
1 cup (235 ml) vegetable broth

1. Wash, peel, and chop or dice the beets. Wash, halve, core, and peel the apples. Cut the apples into thick slices.
2. Rinse the chicken and pat dry with paper towels. Cut into cubes. If desired, lightly sauté the chicken in a hot skillet with a bit of olive oil.
3. Transfer the chicken to the slow cooker and sprinkle on the savory or sweet seasoning combination of your choice. Add the beets, apples, water, and broth. Stir to combine.
4. Cover and cook on low for 6 hours or on high for 4 hours or until a thermometer inserted in the thickest portion of a chicken breast registers 165°F (75°C) and the juices run clear. Remove from the slow cooker and set aside to cool.

Preparation and Storage for Baby

Mash or puree the beets as needed to serve to your baby. Mash a few of the chicken cubes or chop or puree to serve to baby.

Store leftovers in the refrigerator for up to 3 days for babies, up to 5 days for adults.

To freeze, follow the stage three directions in "Freezing Homemade Baby Food" on page 28.

For the Family

It's a meal!

> *Make this recipe savory or sweet; no matter which you choose, it will be a keeper!.*

❄ Freezes well. 🍎 B vitamins, including folate, plus vitamins A, C, and E as well as iron, calcium, fiber, and protein

Classic Slow Cooker Pot Roast

When I made this recipe when my kids were younger, they would wonder why it was called pot roast when I was using the slow cooker. They also wondered what type of meat a "pot roast" could be.

Age and Stage: 8 months+ | Stage Two or Three | Second and Third Foods and Beyond

Slow Cooker Size: 6 quarts (5.7 l); oval

4 large carrots

2 small onions

1 beef chuck roast (3 to 4 pounds [1.4 to 1.8 kg])

1 teaspoon ground pepper

2 tablespoons (30 ml) olive oil

3 cups (710 ml) beef broth, divided

¼ cup (60 ml) Worcestershire sauce

3 ounces (85 g, half of a small can) basil tomato paste

2 teaspoons minced garlic

1 teaspoon dried thyme

1 teaspoon dried oregano

1. Wash, peel, and chop the carrots. Peel and dice the onions.
2. Rinse the roast and pat dry with paper towels. Season on all sides with the pepper. In a skillet, heat the oil over medium-high heat. Add the roast and brown on all sides.
3. Transfer the roast to the slow cooker. Add the carrots and onions. In a bowl or measuring cup, combine 1 cup of the broth with the Worcestershire sauce and tomato paste. Stir or whisk to combine. Pour the mixture into the slow cooker. Add the remaining 2 cups broth, garlic, thyme, and oregano and stir to combine.
4. Cover and cook on low for 8 hours or on high for 4 hours or until a thermometer inserted in the center of the roast registers 160°F (70°C).

Preparation and Storage for Baby

Remove the beef and allow to cool for a few minutes before slicing. Remove the carrots and onions and set aside to cool. Mash or puree the carrots as needed to serve to your baby. Slice a piece of the roast and then dice it into bite-size pieces or mash or puree to serve to baby.

Store leftovers in the refrigerator for up to 3 days for babies, up to 5 days for adults.

To freeze, follow the stage three directions in "Freezing Homemade Baby Food" on page 28.

For the Family

It's a meal!

❄ Freezes well.   🍎 B vitamins, including folate, and A, C, and E, iron, calcium, magnesium, fiber, and protein

Cheesy Chicken and Carrots

The one thing that I recall about serving this recipe when my sons were little? Complete silence at the dinner table. Everyone would rather eat this delicious combo than argue, poke, or prod.

Age and Stage: 8 months+ | Stage Two or Three | Second and Third Foods and Beyond
Slow Cooker Size: 6 quarts (5.7 l); oval

4 large carrots
2 small onions
4 boneless skinless chicken breasts
Pinch of garlic powder
Pinch of ground pepper
1 tablespoon (15 ml) olive oil
¼ cup (60 ml) chicken broth
1 cup (120 g) grated cheddar cheese

1. Wash, peel, and chop the carrots. Peel and dice the onions.
2. Rinse the chicken and pat dry with paper towels. Season with the garlic powder and pepper.
3. Wipe the slow cooker with the oil. Pour the broth into the slow cooker and add the carrots. Place the chicken breasts on top of the carrots and add the onions.
4. Cover and cook on low for 8 hours or on high for 4 hours. After 4 hours (on low) or 2 hours (on high), check the progress of the chicken. Continue cooking until the carrots are tender and a thermometer inserted in the center of a chicken breast registers 165°F (75°C).
5. Sprinkle the cheese over the chicken and vegetables. Cover and let rest for 5 minutes or until the cheese has melted.

Preparation and Storage for Baby

Remove the chicken and allow to cool for a few minutes before dividing into portions. Remove the carrots and onions and set aside to cool. Mash or puree the carrots as needed to serve to your baby. Dice a whole or half of a chicken breast; you can mash or puree it as needed to serve to baby.

Store leftovers in the refrigerator for up to 3 days for babies, up to 5 days for adults.

To freeze, follow the stage three directions in "Freezing Homemade Baby Food" on page 28.

For the Family

It's a meal! Dice the chicken breasts and serve over cooked rice or alongside mashed potatoes. Serve with Caesar salad and some warm, crusty bread.

❄ Freezes well.   🍎 B vitamins, including folate, and A, C, and E, iron, calcium, fiber, and protein

Cinnamon Chicken with Figs and Pears

"Are you getting all Mediterranean on us again, Mom?" said two boys who actually paid attention when this dish was explained long ago.

Age and Stage: 8 months+ | Stage Two or Three | Second and Third Foods and Beyond
Slow Cooker Size: 6 quarts (5.7 l); oval

4 pears, such as Bosc
7 dried figs
½ teaspoon ground cinnamon
½ teaspoon ground pepper
½ teaspoon ground ginger
4 to 6 boneless, skinless chicken breasts
1 tablespoon (15 ml) olive oil
½ cup (120 ml) chicken broth

Conjuring up flavors of the Mediterranean, figs and pears go nicely with the light flavor of chicken. This meal is full of iron and bursting with flavor, too!

1. Wash, halve, core, peel, and roughly chop the pears. Cut the figs in half.
2. In a small bowl, combine the cinnamon, pepper, and ginger. Mix well. Rinse the chicken and pat dry with paper towels. Season with the cinnamon mixture.
3. Wipe the slow cooker with the oil. Pour the broth into the slow cooker and add the chicken. Place the pears and figs on top of the chicken.
4. Cover and cook on low for 8 hours or on high for 4 hours or until a thermometer inserted in the center of a chicken breast registers 165°F (75°C) and the juices run clear.

Preparation and Storage for Baby

Remove the chicken and allow to cool for a few minutes before dividing into portions. Remove the figs and any pears that have not been reduced to a sauce; set aside to cool. Mash or puree the figs and pears as needed to serve to your baby. Dice a whole or half of a chicken breast; you can mash or puree it as needed to serve to baby.

Store leftovers in the refrigerator for up to 3 days for babies, up to 5 days for adults.

To freeze, follow the stage three directions in "Freezing Homemade Baby Food" on page 28.

For the Family

It's a meal! Dice the chicken breasts and serve over cooked jasmine rice or with cinnamon-roasted potatoes. Serve with a mixed garden salad and some warm, crusty bread.

※ Freezes well. ● B vitamins, including folate, plus A, C, and E, iron, calcium, magnesium, fiber, and protein

Lentil and Chicken Stew

Stew over this tasty recipe. Ugh Mom, really?

Age and Stage: 8 months+ | Stage Two or Three | Second and Third Foods and Beyond

Slow Cooker Size: 6 quarts (5.7 l); oval

2 carrots
1 sweet potato
2 red potatoes
¼ cup (40 g) minced onion
2 cloves garlic
½ teaspoon ground turmeric
½ teaspoon ground cumin
½ teaspoon ground pepper
½ teaspoonground ginger
½ teaspoon ground cinnamon
4 boneless, skinless chicken breasts
4 cups (945 ml) chicken broth
1¾ cups (336 g) lentils (brown, red, or yellow)

1. Wash, peel, and roughly chop the carrots, sweet potato, and red potatoes. Peel and finely chop the onion. Peel and mince the garlic.
2. In a small bowl, combine the turmeric, cumin, pepper, ginger, and cinnamon. Mix well. Rinse the chicken and pat dry with paper towels. Dice into bite-size cubes. Season with the turmeric mixture.
3. Pour the broth into the slow cooker and add the lentils. Transfer the chicken to the slow cooker. Top with the vegetables.
4. Cover and cook on low for 5 hours or on high for 2 to 2½ hours or until a thermometer inserted in the center of a chicken breast registers 165°F (75°C) and the juices run clear.

Preparation and Storage for Baby

Remove the chicken and allow to cool for a few minutes before dividing into portions. Remove the potatoes, carrots, and lentils and set aside to cool; mash or puree a portion as needed to serve to your baby. You can mash or puree the chicken as needed to best serve to baby. Combine the lentils and veggies with the chicken and create a meal for your baby or toddler.

Store leftovers in the refrigerator for up to 3 days for babies, up to 5 days for adults.

To freeze, follow the stage three directions in "Freezing Homemade Baby Food" on page 28.

For the Family

It's a stew meal! Serve with salad and warm biscuits or crusty bread.

✳ Freezes well.   🍎 B vitamins, including folate, and A, C, and E, iron, calcium, magnesium, fiber, and protein

Three-Cheese Mac and Cheese

Finally, a recipe that doesn't have meat or veggies and is just plain ooey-gooey good!
Thanks, Mom!

Age and Stage: 8 months+ | Stage Two or Three | Second and Third Foods and Beyond
Slow Cooker Size: 6 quarts (5.7 l); oval

1½ cups (355 ml) chicken or vegetable broth
¼ cup (60 ml) whole milk
¼ cup (40 g) minced onion
1 teaspoon garlic powder
1 teaspoon ground pepper
1 tablespoon (14 g) butter
1 pound (455 g) elbow pasta
½ cup (60 g) grated cheddar cheese
½ cup (60 g) grated monterey jack cheese
½ cup (60 g) grated colby cheese

1. In a bowl or large measuring cup, combine the broth, milk, onion, garlic powder, and pepper.
2. Grease the slow cooker with the butter. Pour the pasta into the slow cooker and add the cheeses. Pour in the broth mixture.
3. Cover and cook on low for 2 to 3 hours, stirring after the first hour.

Preparation and Storage for Baby

Remove the mac and cheese and allow to cool for a few minutes before dividing into portions. It is best to chop or mince the mac and cheese when serving to babies and to cut into bite-sized piece when serving to toddlers.

Store leftovers in the refrigerator for up to 3 days for babies, up to 5 days for adults.

To freeze, follow the stage three directions in "Freezing Homemade Baby Food" on page 28. This dish will not freeze as well as other dishes, and reheating is best done in a saucepan on the stovetop.

For the Family

Serve with any meat dish and a salad and warm biscuits or crusty bread.

❄ Freezes only moderately well.   🍎 B vitamins, including folate, and A, C, and E, plus iron, calcium, magnesium, fiber, and protein   ★ Pastas made from wheat are considered to be allergenic and may not be suitable for those with gluten sensitivities. Milk may not be suitable for those with lactose intolerance. Consult with your pediatrician about food allergies and feeding baby solid foods.

Fiesta Grains

In an earlier recipe, we tasted a bit of the Mediterranean. With this simple but delicious recipe, it's fiesta time!

Age and Stage: 8 months+ | Stage Two or Three | Second and Third Foods and Beyond
Slow Cooker Size: 4 quarts (3.8 l); round

1½ cups (278 g) white long-grain rice
1 small sweet potato
½ green bell pepper
1 small onion
3 cups (710 ml) chicken broth
½ cup (70 g) frozen diced carrots
½ cup (65 g) frozen corn
½ teaspoon ground cumin
½ teaspoon paprika
½ teaspoon ground pepper

1. Rinse and drain the rice. Wash, peel, and roughly chop the sweet potato. Wash, seed, and finely dice the bell pepper. Peel and mince the onion.
2. Pour the broth into the slow cooker. Add the rice and then the sweet potato, bell pepper, onion, carrots, and corn. In a small bowl, combine the cumin, paprika, and pepper. Mix well. Sprinkle over the rice and vegetables.
3. Cover and cook on low for 2 to 3 hours or until tender.

Preparation and Storage for Baby

Allow to cool for a few minutes before dividing into portions.

Store leftovers in the refrigerator for up to 3 days for babies, up to 5 days for adults.

To freeze, follow the stage three directions in "Freezing Homemade Baby Food" on page 28.

For the Family

It's a side dish to be served with any entrée, including baked chicken, apple pork tenderloin, salmon, or any other meat/protein that you like. Add a side veggie, too.

❄ Freezes with mixed results. 🍎 B vitamins, including folate, and A, C, and E, iron, calcium, magnesium, fiber, and protein

Easy Savory Pork Medallions with Fruit Sauce

Everything is better with a fruit sauce on it. You can make this tasty recipe with cranberries or just apples or even peaches. Ask the kids to decide.

Age and Stage: 8 months+ | Stage Two or Three | Second and Third Foods and Beyond
Slow Cooker Size: 6 quarts (5.7 l); oval

4 apples, such as Granny Smith
3 pears, such as Bosc
1 small onion
2 pork tenderloins (1 to 1½ pounds each [455 to 683 g])
½ cup (120 ml) vegetable broth
½ teaspoon ground ginger
½ teaspoon ground pepper
½ teaspoon garlic powder

1. Wash, halve, core, peel, and roughly chop the apples and pears. Peel and mince the onion. Rinse the pork tenderloins and pat dry with paper towels.
2. Pour the broth into the slow cooker. In a small bowl, combine the ginger, pepper, and garlic powder. Mix well. Sprinkle over the broth and stir. Add the tenderloins, apples, pears, and onion. Stir to combine.
3. Cover and cook on low for 6 hours or on high for 3 to 4 hours or until a thermometer inserted in the center of a tenderloin registers 160°F (70°C) and the juices run clear.

Preparation and Storage for Baby

Remove the tenderloins to a plate and let rest and cool before slicing. Remove the fruits and onion; mash together. Slice the tenderloins into medallions. Mash or puree a portion of the tenderloin as needed for your baby and serve with the mashed fruits and onion.

Store leftovers in the refrigerator for up to 3 days for babies, up to 5 days for adults.

To freeze, follow the stage three directions in "Freezing Homemade Baby Food" on page 28.

For the Family

Serve with rice or mashed potatoes; use any remaining juices to spoon over the starch side dish. This goes great with roasted carrots or butternut squash.

❄ Freezes well.   🍎 B vitamins, including folate, and A, C, and E, iron, calcium, magnesium, fiber, and protein

Scalloped Sweet Potatoes with Apples

My favorite scalloped potato is amazing when you use sweet potatoes, nutmeg, cinnamon, and a pinch of ginger. Add shredded cheddar cheese, too!

Age and Stage: 8 months+ | Stage Two or Three | Second and Third Foods and Beyond
Slow Cooker Size: 6 quarts (5.7 l); oval

8 medium sweet potatoes
3 apples, such as Granny Smith
1 tablespoon (15 ml) olive oil
4 tablespoons (56 g) butter
½ cup (63 g) flour
2 cups (475 ml) water
1½ cups (355 ml) chicken broth

2 tablespoons (28 g) mayonnaise
Pinch of salt
Pinch of ground cinnamon
Pinch of ground nutmeg
Pinch of ground ginger
1 cup (120 g) grated cheddar cheese

1. Wash and peel the sweet potatoes. Cut into thin slices. Wash, halve, core, and peel the apples. Cut into thin slices.
2. Grease the slow cooker with the olive oil; be sure to be generous on the bottom of the vessel. Layer the sweet potatoes in the slow cooker, followed by the apples.
3. In a saucepan over medium heat, melt the butter. Whisk in the flour until smooth. Gradually add the water, broth, mayonnaise, salt, cinnamon, nutmeg, and ginger. Cook, whisking frequently, until the mixture is thick and bubbly. Pour the mixture over the apples. Sprinkle with an additional pinch of the cinnamon, nutmeg, and ginger.
4. Cover and cook on low for 4 to 6 hours or on high for 3 hours. Turn off the slow cooker. Sprinkle with the cheddar cheese and allow to rest for 10 minutes.

Preparation and Storage for Baby

Cool before serving to baby. Any dish with a sauce may potentially burn baby, so be sure to check the temperature before serving. Mash or puree the potatoes as needed for your baby's ability and then serve to your baby.

Store leftovers in the refrigerator for up to 3 days for babies, up to 5 days for adults.

To freeze, follow the stage three directions in "Freezing Homemade Baby Food" on page 28.

For the Family

Serve with barbecue chicken, beef brisket, or baby back ribs; this dish also makes a great accompaniment to baked chicken and pork roast.

✳ Freezes well, but thaw and warm in an oven to avoid mushiness. 🍎 B vitamins, including folate, plus A, C, and E, iron, calcium, magnesium, fiber, and protein ★ Note that mayonnaise usually contains eggs. If you or anyone in your family has a history of food allergies, contact your pediatrician about offering your baby foods that may be allergenic.

Chicken with Root Veggies and Pears

"It's amazing that you can toss all of these junky foods into a pot and it comes out tasting good!" said the son who should grow up to be a food critic—or not.

Age and Stage: 8 months+ | Stage Two or Three | Second and Third Foods and Beyond
Slow Cooker Size: 6 quarts (5.7 l); oval

2 carrots
4 parsnips
3 red potatoes
3 pears, such as Bosc
4 boneless, skinless chicken breasts
2 tablespoons (28 g) butter
½ cup (120 ml) chicken broth
Pinch of ground pepper
Pinch of ground cinnamon
Pinch of dried thyme

> *Chicken and root veggies are a classic, but when you add pears, the flavor is earthy and sweet. Delish!*
>
>

1. Wash and peel the carrots, parsnips, and potatoes. Dice into small cubes. Wash, halve, core, and peel the pears. Dice into small cubes. Rinse the chicken and pat dry with paper towels. Cut into 1-inch (2.5 cm) pieces.
2. Lightly grease the slow cooker with the butter. Layer the veggies in the slow cooker. Top with the chicken, followed by the pears. Pour in the broth and sprinkle with the pepper, cinnamon, and thyme.
3. Cover and cook on low for 6 to 8 hours or on high for 4 hours, or until the vegetables are tender and a thermometer inserted in the center of a chicken breast registers 165°F (75°C) and the juices run clear.

Preparation and Storage for Baby

Remove a portion of chicken and veggies (the pears will likely have melted in) and set aside to cool. Mash or puree the foods as needed to serve to your baby. You could mash them together or separately. The chicken dices should be tender enough to squish and serve as finger foods.

Store leftovers in the refrigerator for up to 3 days for babies, up to 5 days for adults.

To freeze, follow the stage three directions in "Freezing Homemade Baby Food" on page 28.

For the Family

You can serve this meal as a stew or over rice. My family likes to eat it as a stew and have a salad and biscuits as sides.

❄ Freezes well.   🍎 B vitamins, including folate, and A, C, and E, plus iron, calcium, magnesium, fiber, and protein

Classic Meatballs

What can we say about meatballs other than *easy* and *yummy*? Unfortunately, meatballs look like balls and can sail across the table easily when tiny diners decide to give their pitching arm a workout.

Age and Stage: 8 months+ | Stage Two or Three | Second and Third Foods and Beyond
Slow Cooker Size: 6 quarts (5.7 l); oval

1 carrot

3 Roma (plum) tomatoes

1 teaspoon ground pepper

1 teaspoon dried oregano

1 teaspoon dried basil

1 teaspoon dried thyme

2 pounds (907 g) 90% lean ground beef

1¾ cups (200 g) breadcrumbs

2 eggs, beaten

1 clove garlic, minced

1 tablespoon (15 ml) olive oil

1 can (6 ounces [170 g]) tomato paste

1 can (32 ounces [905 g]) crushed tomatoes

1. Wash, peel, and grate the carrot. Wash and chop the Roma tomatoes. In a small bowl, combine the pepper, oregano, basil, and thyme.
2. In a large bowl, combine the ground beef, breadcrumbs, eggs, garlic, carrot, and half of the herb mixture. Mix together thoroughly. Shape the mixture into about 16 balls.
3. Lightly grease the slow cooker with the olive oil. Add the meatballs and Roma tomatoes. In a medium bowl, combine the tomato paste and crushed tomatoes. Pour the mixture into the slow cooker. Sprinkle with the remaining herb mixture.
4. Cover and cook on low for 6 hours or on high for 4 hours or until the meatballs are no longer pink.

Preparation and Storage for Baby

Remove a few meatballs and set aside to cool. Mash or puree the meatballs, adding a bit of the tomato sauce from the slow cooker if desired. Alternately, you could just dice or squish the meatballs and serve as finger foods; serve with cooked rice for a great pick-up meal.

Store leftovers in the refrigerator for up to 3 days for babies, up to 5 days for adults.

To freeze, follow the stage three directions in "Freezing Homemade Baby Food" on page 28.

For the Family

Serve with your choice of pasta and a salad, or make a meatball sub sandwich.

Meatballs freeze great, taste great, and are the perfect finger food for babies who are learning to self-feed; plus, meatballs are easy to clean up!

❄ Freezes well.   ● B vitamins, including folate, and A, C, and E, iron, calcium, magnesium, fiber, and protein
★ This recipe contains eggs and wheat, which are considered to be highly allergenic. Consult with your pediatrician about food allergies and feeding baby solid foods.

Chicken and Apple Meatballs

Not your typical meatballs, these have a wonderful sweet taste and are a nice break from regular Italian-style meatballs. The addition of apples and cheddar cheese is sure to please all of your diners!

Age and Stage: 8 months+ | Stage Two or Three | Second and Third Foods and Beyond
Slow Cooker Size: 6 quarts (5.7 l); oval

5 small apples
2 pounds (907 g) ground chicken
1½ cups (175 g) breadcrumbs
1 cup (120 g) grated cheddar cheese (optional)
2 eggs
Pinch of ground cinnamon
1 tablespoon (15 ml) olive oil

1. Wash, halve, core, peel, and grate the apples.
2. In a large bowl, combine the apples, ground chicken, breadcrumbs, cheese (if using), eggs, and cinnamon. Mix together thoroughly. Form the mixture into balls about the size of golf balls (1 to 2 inches).
3. Lightly grease the slow cooker with the olive oil. Add the meatballs.
4. Cover and cook on low for 6 hours or until the meatballs are no longer pink.

Preparation and Storage for Baby

Remove the meatballs from the slow cooker and set aside to cool. Mash or cut up a portion of the meatballs to serve to your baby.

Store leftovers in the refrigerator for up to 3 days for babies, up to 5 days for adults.

To freeze, follow the stage three directions in "Freezing Homemade Baby Food" on page 28.

For the Family

Serve meatballs with a pasta dish, make meatball sandwiches, or serve as appetizers.

❄ Freezes well. ● B vitamins, including folate, and A, C, and E, iron, calcium, magnesium, fiber, and protein
★ This recipe contains eggs, cheese, and wheat, which are considered to be highly allergenic. If you or anyone in your family has a history of food allergies, contact your pediatrician about offering your baby foods that may be allergenic.

Creamy Dill Salmon with Peas

A conversation in my kitchen:

"Fish again?"

"It's been over a week, but yes, fish again. It's yummy and good for your brain."

"My brain is just fine, thanks."

Age and Stage: 8 months+ | Stage Two or Three | Second and Third Foods and Beyond

Slow Cooker Size: 6 quarts (5.7 l); oval

1 salmon fillet (2 to 3 pounds [907 g to 1.4 kg]), skinned
2 tablespoons (28 g) butter
1 cup (130 g) frozen peas
4 ounces (115 g) trimmed dill fronds (just the frilly parts)
½ cup (115 g) plain whole milk yogurt
½ cup (120 ml) vegetable broth
Pinch of ground pepper
Pinch of garlic powder

1. Rinse the salmon and pat it dry with paper towels.
2. Lightly grease the slow cooker with the butter. Transfer the salmon to the slow cooker and add the peas. Place the dill on top of the salmon. In a small bowl, whisk together the yogurt and broth. Cover the salmon with the yogurt mixture and sprinkle with the pepper and garlic powder.
3. Cover and cook on low for 3 hours or until the salmon is opaque and flakes easily with a fork.

Preparation and Storage for Baby

Remove the salmon and peas from the slow cooker and set aside a portion to cool for baby. Mash or puree as needed to serve to your baby. You could mash the salmon and peas together or separately. They should be tender enough to squish and serve as finger foods.

Store leftovers in the refrigerator for up to 3 days for babies, up to 5 days for adults.

To freeze, follow the stage three directions in "Freezing Homemade Baby Food" on page 28.

For the Family

This recipe is delicious served with rice and a salad.

❋ Freezes well. ● B vitamins, including folate, and A, C, and E, iron, calcium, magnesium, fiber, and protein
★ This recipe contains yogurt; dairy products can be allergenic for some people. If you or anyone in your family has a history of food allergies, contact your pediatrician about offering your baby foods that may be allergenic.

Beef Stew

Stew is a word that sounds funny to kids, and it is a dish that allows developing babies and toddlers to use their fingers to pinch and grasp a variety of colorful and tasty foods. This beef stew recipe is the first of three stews that will have your kiddos pinching and eating away!

Age and Stage: 8 months+ | Stage Two or Three | Second and Third Foods and Beyond
Slow Cooker Size: 6 quarts (5.7 l); oval

2 carrots
2 russet potatoes
2 pounds (907 g) stew beef, cubed
¼ cup (31 g) flour
Ground pepper, to taste
Garlic powder, to taste

Dried oregano, to taste
Paprika, to taste
2 tablespoons (28 g) butter
1 cup (130 g) frozen peas
1½ cups (355 ml) beef broth
1 tablespoon (15 ml) Worcestershire sauce

1. Wash and peel the carrots. Dice into small cubes. Wash and peel the potatoes. Dice into small cubes. Rinse the beef and pat dry with paper towels. Cut into 1-inch (2.5 cm) pieces, if needed.
2. In a resealable plastic bag, combine the flour and a pinch of pepper, garlic powder, oregano, and paprika. Add the beef cubes, seal the bag, and toss until the cubes are evenly coated.
3. Lightly grease the slow cooker with the butter. Add the beef, carrots, potatoes, and peas. In a measuring cup, combine the broth and Worcestershire sauce. Pour the broth mixture into the slow cooker. If desired, sprinkle with another pinch of pepper, garlic powder, oregano, and paprika. Stir to combine.
4. Cover and cook on low for 8 hours or on high for 4 hours or until the vegetables are tender and the beef is no longer pink.

Preparation and Storage for Baby

Remove a portion of the beef and veggies for your baby and set aside to cool. Mash or puree the foods as needed to serve to your baby. You could mash them together or separately. The beef dices should be tender enough to squish and serve as finger foods.

Store leftovers in the refrigerator for up to 3 days for babies, up to 5 days for adults.

To freeze, follow the stage three directions in "Freezing Homemade Baby Food" on page 28.

For the Family

This is a stew meal. Serve with rice or egg noodles if you like, and bake some biscuits and make a salad.

❄ Freezes well. ♠ B vitamins, including folate, and A, C, and E, plus iron, calcium, magnesium, fiber, and protein
★ This recipe contains wheat, which is considered to be highly allergenic for some people. If you or anyone in your family has a history of food allergies, contact your pediatrician about offering your baby foods that may be allergenic

Chicken Stew

Chicken stew is a great way to toss all your favorites into the slow cooker and have a warm, hearty meal at the end of the day. Like the beef stew recipe, the ingredients in this dish are great for finger foods and will help with the pincer grasp and hand–eye coordination. And you thought this was just a meal!

Age and Stage: 8 months+ | Stage Two or Three | Second and Third Foods and Beyond
Slow Cooker Size: 6 quarts (5.7 l); oval

2 carrots
2 russet potatoes
2 pounds (907 g) boneless,
  skinless chicken breasts
¼ cup (31 g) flour
Ground pepper, to taste
Garlic powder, to taste

Dried rosemary, to taste
Dried thyme, to taste
Paprika, to taste
2 tablespoons (28 g) butter
1 cup (130 g) frozen peas
1½ cups (355 ml) chicken broth

1. Wash and peel the carrots. Dice into small cubes. Wash and peel the potatoes. Dice into small cubes. Rinse the chicken and pat dry with paper towels. Cut into 1-inch (2.5 cm) pieces.
2. In a resealable plastic bag, combine the flour and a pinch of pepper, garlic powder, rosemary, thyme, paprika. Add the chicken, seal the bag, and toss until the chicken is evenly coated.
3. Lightly grease the slow cooker with the butter. Add the chicken, carrots, potatoes, peas, and broth. If desired, sprinkle with another pinch of pepper, garlic powder, rosemary, thyme, and paprika. Stir to combine.
4. Cover and cook on low for 8 hours or on high for 4 hours or until the vegetables are tender and the chicken is no longer pink.

Preparation and Storage for Baby

Remove a portion of the chicken and veggies for your baby and set aside to cool. Mash or puree the foods as needed to serve to your baby. You could mash them together or separately. The chicken should be tender enough to squish and serve as finger foods.

Store leftovers in the refrigerator for up to 3 days for babies, up to 5 days for adults.

To freeze, follow the stage three directions in "Freezing Homemade Baby Food" on page 28.

For the Family

This is a stew meal. Serve with rice or egg noodles if you like, and bake some biscuits and make a salad.

❄ Freezes well.   🍎 B vitamins, including folate, and A, C, and E, iron, calcium, magnesium, fiber, and protein
★ This recipe contains wheat, which is considered to be highly allergenic for some people. If you or anyone in your family has a history of food allergies, contact your pediatrician about offering your baby foods that may be allergenic.

Fish Stew

Yes, it's fish, again! But, this time, the fish is in a tasty stew recipe that your kiddos will find very intriguing. Finding ways to serve fish to kids is not often easy, but this is one stew that is sure to please!

Age and Stage: 8 months+ | Stage Two or Three | Second and Third Foods and Beyond
Slow Cooker Size: 6 quarts (5.7 l); oval

2 carrots
2 russet potatoes
2 pounds (907 g) haddock or cod, skinned and cut into large cubes or chunks
¼ cup (31 g) flour
Ground pepper, to taste
Garlic powder, to taste
Dried dillweed, to taste
2 tablespoons (28 g) butter
1 cup (130 g) frozen peas
1½ cups (355 ml) vegetable broth

1. Wash and peel the carrots. Dice into small cubes. Wash and peel the potatoes. Dice into small cubes. Rinse the fish and pat dry with paper towels. Cut into 1-inch (2.5 cm) pieces.
2. In a resealable plastic bag, combine the flour and a pinch of pepper, garlic powder, and dillweed. Add the fish, seal the bag, and toss until the fish is evenly coated.
3. Lightly grease the slow cooker with the butter. Add the fish, carrots, potatoes, peas, and broth. If desired, sprinkle with another pinch of pepper, garlic powder, and dillweed. Stir to combine.
4. Cover and cook on low for 6 hours or on high for 3 hours or until the vegetables are tender and the fish flakes easily.

Preparation and Storage for Baby

Remove a portion of the fish and veggies and set aside to cool. Mash or puree the foods as needed to serve to your baby. You could mash them together or separately. The fish should be tender enough to squish and serve as finger foods.

Store leftovers in the refrigerator for up to 3 days for babies, up to 5 days for adults.

To freeze, follow the stage three directions in "Freezing Homemade Baby Food" on page 28.

For the Family

This is a stew meal. Serve with rice or egg noodles if you like, and bake some biscuits and make a salad.

> *Get your omega-3s in this tasty stew full of nutritious veggies and broth.*

❄ Freezes well.   🍎 B vitamins, including folate, and A, C, and E, iron, calcium, magnesium, fiber, and protein
★ This recipe contains wheat, which is considered to be highly allergenic for some people. If you or anyone in your family has a history of food allergies, contact your pediatrician about offering your baby foods that may be allergenic.

Tropical Chicken and Rice Noodles

A taste of the tropics. Yes, dear, pineapple does belong with chicken!

Age and Stage: 8 months+ | Stage Two or Three | Second and Third Foods and Beyond
Slow Cooker Size: 6 quarts (5.7 l); oval

2 sweet potatoes
2 pounds (907 g) boneless, skinless chicken breasts
1 cup (155 g) diced pineapple
1 cup (175 g) diced mango
1 cup (130 g) frozen peas
2 cups (475 ml) vegetable broth
½ teaspoon ground pepper
½ teaspoon ground ginger
7 ounces (200 g, half of a 14-ounce package) rice noodles

1. Wash and peel the sweet potatoes. Dice into small cubes. Rinse the chicken and pat dry with paper towels. Cut into 1-inch (2.5 cm) pieces. If desired, brown the chicken in a hot skillet with a bit of olive oil.
2. Transfer the raw or browned chicken to the slow cooker. Add the pineapple, mango, sweet potatoes, and peas. Pour in the broth and add the pepper and ginger.
3. Cover and cook on low for 4 hours. Add the noodles and continue to cook for 1 hour or until the chicken is no longer pink.

Preparation and Storage for Baby

Remove a portion of the chicken, sweet potatoes, noodles, and fruits and set aside to cool. Mash or puree the foods as needed to serve to your baby. You could mash them together or separately. The chicken and fruit and sweet potato cubes should be tender enough to squish and serve as finger foods. Cut the noodles into manageable pieces for your child.

Store leftovers in the refrigerator for up to 3 days for babies, up to 5 days for adults.

To freeze, follow the stage three directions in "Freezing Homemade Baby Food" on page 28.

For the Family

It's a meal! Serve with warm pita.

❄ Freezes well. 🍎 B vitamins, including folate, and A, C, and E, iron, calcium, magnesium, fiber, and protein

Figgy Pork with Apple Butter

Apple butter is great on pancakes to be sure, but it's also a great accompaniment to many other dishes, including this figgy pork tenderloin.

Age and Stage: 8 months+ | Stage Two or Three | Second and Third Foods and Beyond

Slow Cooker Size: 6 quarts (5.7 l); oval

1 pork tenderloin

3 figs, stems removed

2 cups (500 g) apple butter (see below)

1. Rinse the tenderloin and pat dry with paper towels. Rinse the figs and pat dry with paper towels. Chop the figs.
2. Place the tenderloin in the slow cooker and add the figs. Cover the tenderloin with the apple butter.
3. Cover and cook on low for 6 hours or until a thermometer inserted in the center of the tenderloin registers 160°F (70°C) and the juices run clear.

Preparation and Storage for Baby

Remove the tenderloin and set aside to cool. Cut a slice or two off of the tenderloin. Mash, puree, or dice as needed to serve to your baby. The tenderloin should be tender enough to squish and serve as finger foods.

Store leftovers in the refrigerator for up to 3 days for babies, up to 5 days for adults.

To freeze, follow the stage three directions in "Freezing Homemade Baby Food" on page 28.

For the Family

Serve with mashed potatoes and butternut squash.

Apple Butter

Slow Cooker Size: 4 to 6 quarts (3.8 to 5.7 l); round or oval

5 pounds (2.3 kg) mixed apples, such as McIntosh, Gala, and Fuji

¼ cup (60 ml) cold water

¼ cup (80 g) maple syrup

¼ cup (60 g) packed brown sugar

1 tablespoon (7 g) ground cinnamon

1 teaspoon ground nutmeg

1 teaspoon ground ginger

2 teaspoons vanilla extract

1. Wash, halve, core, and peel the apples. Cut into slices (or use an apple slicer).
2. Transfer the apple slices to the slow cooker. Add the water, maple syrup, brown sugar, cinnamon, nutmeg, ginger, and vanilla. Stir to combine.
3. Cover and cook on low for 4 hours. Using a potato masher, mash the apples right in the slow cooker. Continue to cook for an additional 4 to 6 hours or until the apples have been reduced to a thick butter texture and the mixture is brown. Mash until smooth. Remove from the slow cooker and set aside to cool. When cool, transfer to storage containers.

❄ Freezes well.   🍎 B vitamins, including folate, and A, C, and E, iron, calcium, magnesium, fiber, and protein

Chicken with Sweet Potatoes and Black Beans

This is a great "treasure-hunting" recipe for kiddos practicing their finger skills. There are so many colors and textures in this dish that your kiddo will enjoy picking out the black beans, sweet potatoes, and chicken.

Age and Stage: 8 months+ | Stage Two or Three | Second and Third Foods and Beyond
Slow Cooker Size: 4 to 6 quarts (3.8 to 5.7 l); oval

1 pound (455 g) dried black beans	3 cups (710 ml) water
2 large sweet potatoes	½ teaspoon garlic powder
1 small onion	½ teaspoon ground pepper
6 boneless, skinless chicken breasts	½ teaspoon ground cumin
3 cups (710 ml) chicken broth	Shredded cheddar cheese, for topping

1. Place the beans in a bowl, cover with water, and soak for at least 5 hours. Drain the beans, transfer to a saucepan, cover with water, and boil for 10 minutes. Drain the water. Rinse the beans and pick through them for any debris.
2. Wash and peel the sweet potatoes. Roughly chop into small but relatively uniform chunks. Peel and mince the onion. Rinse the chicken and pat dry with paper towels. Dice into uniform pieces.
3. Transfer the beans to the slow cooker. Add the sweet potatoes, onion, and chicken. Pour in the broth and water. Add the garlic powder, pepper, and cumin. Stir to combine.
4. Cover and cook on low for 6 hours, checking after 3 hours and adding more water if needed. After 6 hours, recheck. If the chicken is no longer pink and the sweet potatoes and beans are soft, remove the food from the slow cooker and set aside to cool. Otherwise, cook for an additional 1 to 2 hours (to finish cooking more quickly, set the slow cooker to high). Top individual servings with shredded cheddar cheese.

Preparation and Storage for Baby

Remove some of the chicken, beans, and sweet potatoes and set aside to cool. Mash, puree, or dice as needed to serve to your baby. You could mash them together or separately. All of the foods should be tender enough to squish and serve as finger foods.

Store leftovers in the refrigerator for up to 3 days for babies, up to 5 days for adults.

To freeze, follow the stage three directions in "Freezing Homemade Baby Food" on page 28.

For the Family

This is a meal by itself, but it is also nice when served over rice.

Note that the black beans in this recipe may cause baby to have some gassiness.

❄ Freezes well, but you may see some ice crystals. Some separation may occur when thawed; mix to combine.
● B vitamins, including folate, and A and C, fiber, iron, and calcium

Butternut Squash with Apples and Chicken

"How many ways can you think up to make us eat butternut squash?" my son once asked. Rest assured, my little dears, there are a million ways to serve butternut squash to kids!

Age and Stage: 8 months+ | Stage Two or Three | Second and Third Foods and Beyond

Slow Cooker Size: 4 to 6 quarts (3.8 to 5.7 l); oval

1 butternut squash
5 large apples, such as McIntosh
4 boneless, skinless chicken breasts
1 cup (235 ml) chicken broth
¼ teaspoon ground cinnamon
¼ teaspoon dried sage
¼ teaspoon dried rosemary
¼ teaspoon dried thyme

1. Wash the butternut squash. Cut it in half and scoop out the seeds (set them aside to roast, if you'd like). Peel and then roughly chop the squash into relatively uniform chunks. Wash, halve, core, and peel the apples. Roughly chop. Rinse the chicken and pat dry with paper towels. Dice into uniform pieces.
2. Transfer the squash to the slow cooker. Add the apples and chicken. Pour in the broth. Add the cinnamon, sage, rosemary, and thyme. Stir to combine.
3. Cover and cook on low for 5 hours. Check the texture of the squash. The squash will likely be the last ingredient to thoroughly cook, so if it is soft and the chicken is no longer pink, remove the food from the slow cooker and set aside to cool. Otherwise, cook for an additional 2 to 3 hours, checking often (to finish cooking more quickly, set the slow cooker to high).

Preparation and Storage for Baby

Remove some of the chicken, squash, and apples and set aside to cool. Mash, puree, or dice as needed to serve to your baby. You could mash them together or separately. All of the foods should be tender enough to squish and serve as finger foods.

Store leftovers in the refrigerator for up to 3 days for babies, up to 5 days for adults.

To freeze, follow the stage three directions in "Freezing Homemade Baby Food" on page 28.

For the Family

This is a complete meal, but it is also nice when served with rice or roasted potatoes.

❄ Freezes well. 🍎 B vitamins, including folate, and A, C, and E, plus iron, calcium, magnesium, fiber, and protein

Sweet Potato Rice Apple Meatballs

These meatballs are so good that your kids may want to eat them for breakfast!

Age and Stage: 8 months+ | Stage Two or Three | Second and Third Foods and Beyond
Slow Cooker Size: 4 to 6 quarts (3.8 to 5.7 l); oval

1 pound (455 g) ground beef or turkey
1½ cups (248 g) cooked rice (use a sticky rice such as short-grain brown, Arborio, or sushi rice)
½ cup (113 g) mashed sweet potatoes
½ cup (125 g) applesauce
½ teaspoon ground cinnamon
¼ cup (60 ml) apple juice

1. In a bowl, combine the ground beef or turkey, rice, sweet potatoes, applesauce, and cinnamon. Shape the mixture into 1- to 2-inch (2.5 to 5 cm) balls (about the size of a golf ball).
2. Pour the apple juice into the slow cooker. Add the meatballs.
3. Cover and cook on low for 4 hours or until the meatballs are no longer pink.

Preparation and Storage for Baby

Remove the meatballs and set aside to cool. Mash or puree a portion as needed to serve to your baby.

Store leftovers in the refrigerator for up to 3 days for babies, up to 5 days for adults.

To freeze, follow the stage three directions in "Freezing Homemade Baby Food" on page 28.

For the Family

These meatballs reheat well in the microwave or oven, so they're great for a starter or as a snack.

❄ Freezes well.   🍎 B vitamins, including folate, and A, C, and E, iron, calcium, magnesium, fiber, and protein.

Butternut Squash Soup

"How many ways can you think up to make us eat butternut squash?" Rest assured, my little dears, there are a million *and one* ways to serve butternut squash to kids!

Age and Stage: 8 months+ | Stage Two or Three | Second and Third Foods and Beyond
Slow Cooker Size: 4 to 6 quarts (3.8 to 5.7 l); oval

2 butternut squash
1 carrot
1 small sweet onion, such as vidalia
2 cups (475 ml) chicken broth
½ cup (125 g) applesauce
½ teaspoon ground cinnamon
½ teaspoon ground cumin
½ cup (120 ml) coconut milk

1. Wash the butternut squash. Cut them in half and scoop out the seeds (set them aside to roast, if you'd like). Peel and then roughly chop the squash into relatively uniform chunks. Wash peel, and roughly chop the carrot. Peel and mince the onion.
2. Transfer the squash, onion, and carrot to the slow cooker. Pour in the broth. Add the applesauce, cinnamon, and cumin. Stir to combine.
3. Cover and cook on low for 8 hours or until all of the vegetables are tender. Turn off the slow cooker and allow to cool for 10 minutes. Using a hand mixer or immersion blender, puree the mixture into a soup, adding the coconut milk as you go.

Preparation and Storage for Baby

As much as this will pain you due to the mess, offer your baby a small bowl of the soup and give her a spoon. This is a tasty way for baby to get some spoon practice. This soup is also great to use as a sauce; drizzle it over diced chicken or turkey.

Store leftovers in the refrigerator for up to 3 days for babies, up to 5 days for adults.

To freeze, follow the stage three directions in "Freezing Homemade Baby Food" on page 28.

For the Family

Serve this soup with warm, crusty bread and a salad while the snow is gently falling or the rain is whipping and the wind is howling. Add a pinch of paprika or cayenne pepper and top with a dollop of sour cream before serving.

❄ Freezes well. 🍎 B vitamins, including folate, and A, C, and E, iron, calcium, magnesium, fiber, and protein

Creamy, Cheesy Cauliflower Soup

If you don't tell your children this is cauliflower, they never will know. Sometimes it is okay to be a bit vague about a food, especially as your kids get older. Hopefully, when they get older and their friends complain about having to eat "that gross cauliflower," your kids won't be able to relate at all!

Age and Stage: 8 months+ | Stage Two or Three | Second and Third Foods and Beyond
Slow Cooker Size: 4 to 6 quarts (3.8 to 5.7 l); oval

- 1 head cauliflower
- 1 small sweet onion, such as vidalia
- 2 tablespoons (20 g) minced garlic
- 4 cups (945 ml) chicken or vegetable broth
- ½ teaspoon ground pepper
- 2 cups (240 g) grated cheddar cheese
- 1 cup (230 g) plain Greek yogurt, at room temperature

1. Remove the leaves and stem from the cauliflower. Wash the cauliflower and dry with paper towels. Roughly chop. Peel and mince the onion.
2. Add the cauliflower, onion, and garlic to the slow cooker. Pour in the broth. Add the pepper. Stir to combine.
3. Cover and cook on low for 8 hours or until the cauliflower is tender. Either transfer the mixture to a blender or food processor and puree until smooth, or use a hand mixer or immersion blender and puree right inside the slow cooker. Add the cheddar cheese and stir until melted. Stir in the yogurt.

Preparation and Storage for Baby

Ladle a small portion into a bowl or onto a plate and serve to your kiddo. Offer a spoon, but don't get upset when your little one uses her fingers. Be sure that the cheese has thoroughly melted so that there is no choking hazard.

Store leftovers in the refrigerator for up to 3 days for babies, up to 5 days for adults.

To freeze, follow the stage three directions in "Freezing Homemade Baby Food" on page 28.

For the Family

Serve this soup with a roasted turkey and cranberry panini and a salad.

❄ Freezes well.   ● B vitamins, including folate, and A, C, and E, plus iron, calcium, magnesium, fiber, and protein
★ This recipe contains cheese and yogurt; dairy products can be allergenic for some people. If you or anyone in your family has a history of food allergies, contact your pediatrician about offering your baby foods that may be allergenic.

Chicken and Corn Chowder

This chowder is yet another tasty finger food trove of treasures for your little one to pick up. "Look, Mom, squash the corn and it flies through the air."

Age and Stage: 8 months+ | Stage Two or Three | Second and Third Foods and Beyond
Slow Cooker Size: 4 to 6 quarts (3.8 to 5.7 l); oval

2 carrots
1 rib celery
1 small sweet onion, such as vidalia
4 boneless, skinless chicken breasts
2 tablespoons (20 g) minced garlic
1 cup (130 g) frozen or canned and drained corn
1 can (14.75 ounces [417 g]) cream-style corn
4 cups (945 ml) chicken or vegetable broth
½ teaspoon ground pepper
½ teaspoon paprika
1 cup (230 g) plain Greek yogurt, at room temperature (optional)

1. Wash, peel, and roughly chop the carrots. Wash and dice the celery. Peel and mince the onion. Rinse the chicken and pat dry with paper towels. Dice into 1-inch (2.5 cm) pieces.
2. Transfer the chicken, carrots, celery, onion, and garlic to the slow cooker. Add both types of corn. Pour in the broth. Add the pepper and paprika. Stir to combine.
3. Cover and cook on low for 6 to 8 hours or until the vegetables are tender and the chicken is no longer pink. If desired, stir in the yogurt to make a creamier chowder.

Preparation and Storage for Baby

Ladle a small portion into a bowl or onto a plate and serve to your kiddo. Offer a spoon or even a fork, but don't get upset when your little one uses his fingers. Be sure that the chicken and veggies are tender enough to smoosh easily.

Store leftovers in the refrigerator for up to 3 days for babies, up to 5 days for adults.

To freeze, follow the stage three directions in "Freezing Homemade Baby Food" on page 28.

For the Family

Serve this soup with honey corn bread and a crisp garden salad.

※ Freezes well. ● B vitamins, including folate, and A, C, and E, plus iron, calcium, magnesium, fiber, and protein
★ This recipe contains cheese and yogurt; dairy products can be allergenic for some people. If you or anyone in your family has a history of food allergies, contact your pediatrician about offering your baby foods that may be allergenic.

Italian Wedding Soup

"Meatballs in soup—that's a great idea!" said every little kid I know.

Age and Stage: 8 months+ | Stage Two or Three | Second and Third Foods and Beyond

Slow Cooker Size: 4 to 6 quarts (3.8 to 5.7 l); oval

MEATBALLS

1 pound (455 g) ground beef or turkey

1 egg

½ cup (60 g) dried breadcrumbs

½ teaspoon dried oregano,

½ teaspoon dried basil

½ teaspoon ground pepper

SOUP

1 carrot

1 rib celery

1 small sweet onion, such as Vidalia

1½ cups (210 g) diced or shredded cooked chicken breasts

2 tablespoons (20 g) minced garlic

8 cups (1.9 l) chicken broth

Pinch of dried oregano

Pinch of dried basil

Pinch of ground pepper

2 cups (70 g) chopped spinach

¼ cup (45 g) acini di pepe pasta (for older babies and toddlers, this is a nice bite-size pasta)

Grated Parmesan cheese (optional)

1. *To make the meatballs:* Preheat the oven to 350°F. Place a fine wire rack inside a rimmed sheet pan.
2. In a medium bowl, combine the beef or turkey, egg, breadcrumbs, oregano, basil, and pepper. Shape the mixture into small meatballs and place on the rack.
3. Bake for 10 to 15 minutes, or until no longer pink. Transfer to a plate lined with paper towels to drain.
4. *To make the soup:* Wash and the carrot and celery. Peel the carrot and roughly chop. Roughly chop the celery. Peel and finely chop the onion.
5. Add the meatballs, chicken, carrot, celery, onion, and garlic to the slow cooker. Pour in the broth. Add the oregano, basil, and pepper. Stir to combine.
6. Cover and cook on low for 6 to 8 hours. When there's 1 hour of cooking time left, add the spinach and pasta. Sprinkle individual servings with Parmesan cheese, if desired.

Preparation and Storage for Baby

Ladle a small portion into a bowl for your kiddo and offer him a spoon. This soup won't be thick enough to serve on a plate; however, you can use a slotted spoon to serve some of the chicken, meatballs, pasta, and veggies and then spoon some of the broth on top. Try not to get upset when your little one uses his fingers. Be sure that the chicken and veggies are tender enough to smoosh easily.

Store leftovers in the refrigerator for up to 3 days for babies, up to 5 days for adults.

To freeze, follow the stage three directions in "Freezing Homemade Baby Food" on page 28.

For the Family

Serve this soup as a starter to an Italian dinner or with homemade calzones and caesar salad.

❄ Freezes well. ● B vitamins, including folate, as well as A, C, and E, plus iron, calcium, magnesium, fiber, and protein

Chicken and Rice Soup

Chicken and rice is a classic combination that can be cooked in many different ways. This soup is almost like a casserole, with the same big flavor and creamy goodness. And, yes, there are even some chunks of chicken and vegetables that little fingers can pick up and self-feed from a bowl or plate. Winner winner!

Age and Stage: 8 months+ | Stage Two or Three | Second and Third Foods and Beyond
Slow Cooker Size: 4 to 6 quarts (3.8 to 5.7 l); oval

2 carrots
2 ribs celery
1 small sweet onion, such as vidalia
4 boneless, skinless chicken breasts
2 tablespoons (20 g) minced garlic
1 cup (190 g) brown rice
8 cups (1.9 l) chicken or vegetable broth
½ teaspoon dried rosemary
½ teaspoon dried thyme
½ teaspoon dried sage
½ teaspoon ground pepper
½ teaspoon paprika

1. Wash, peel, and roughly chop the carrots. Wash and dice the celery. Peel and mince the onion. Rinse the chicken and pat dry with paper towels. Cut each breast in half.
2. Transfer the chicken, carrots, celery, onion, and garlic to the slow cooker. Add the rice. Pour in the broth. Add the rosemary, thyme, sage, pepper, and paprika. Stir to combine.
3. Cover and cook on low for 6 to 8 hours or until the vegetables are tender and the chicken is no longer pink.

Preparation and Storage for Baby

Ladle a small portion into a bowl for your kiddo and offer him a spoon. This soup will not be thick enough to serve on a plate; however, you can use a slotted spoon to serve some of the chicken, rice, and veggies and then spoon some of the broth on top. Again, try not to get upset when your little one uses his fingers. Be sure that the chicken and veggies are tender enough to smoosh easily.

Store leftovers in the refrigerator for up to 3 days for babies, up to 5 days for adults.

To freeze, follow the stage three directions in "Freezing Homemade Baby Food" on page 28.

For the Family

Serve this soup with tomato and grilled cheese sandwiches with a crisp garden salad.

❋ Freezes well.   ● B vitamins, including folate, and A, C, and E, plus iron, calcium, magnesium, fiber, and protein

Sample Meal Plans

Stage One Sample Meal Plan

Stage 1*	Sunday	Monday	Tuesday	Wednesday	Thursday	Friday	Saturday
Week 1	1 teaspoon mashed avocado	1 teaspoon mashed avocado	1 teaspoon mashed avocado	1 teaspoon mashed banana	1 teaspoon mashed banana	1 teaspoon mashed banana	1 teaspoon banana and avocado mashed together
Week 2	1 teaspoon Slow Cooker Apples (page 48)/ applesauce	1 teaspoon Slow Cooker Apples (page 48)/ applesauce	1 teaspoon Slow Cooker Apples (page 48)/ applesauce	1 teaspoon banana and Slow Cooker Apples (page 48)/apple-sauce mashed together	1 teaspoon avocado and Slow Cooker Apples (page 48)/ applesauce mashed together	1 teaspoon Diced Butternut Squash (page 189)	1 teaspoon Diced Butternut Squash (page 189)
Week 3	1 teaspoon Diced Butternut Squash (page 189)	1 teaspoon Sweet Potatoes (page 73)	1 teaspoon Slow Cooker Apples (page 48)/ applesauce and Sweet Potatoes (page 73) mashed together	1 teaspoon Sweet Potatoes (page 73)	1 teaspoon oatmeal	1 teaspoon oatmeal	1 teaspoon oatmeal and banana mashed together

*Typically, babies 6 to 8 months old are considered to be in stage one, but this stage may also include babies as young as 4 months who begin solid foods.

Above are examples of how you might choose to begin your baby on solid foods. Note that we've introduced only one new food at a time and waited 3 days before introducing the next new food. This way, if baby has any allergies or other reactions, it will be easier to determine which food is the culprit.

Offer your baby her regular milk feedings before giving her solid foods. Milk is still most important from a nutritional standpoint at this stage. (See "Suggested Daily Breast-Feeding or Formula-Feeding Schedule" page 203.) Start feeding baby 1 or 2 teaspoons of solid food once per day and gradually increase to 1 tablespoon. Additional meals are usually added after baby has been eating solid foods for 3 to 4 weeks. Note that you don't have to strictly follow this schedule and should offer your baby as much as she will eat.

Stages Two and Three Sample Meal Plan

Stage 2 and 3*	Sunday	Monday	Tuesday	Wednesday	Thursday	Friday	Saturday
Breakfast							
Cereal**	Overnight Apple Oatmeal (page 143)	Kamut (page 151)	1 teaspoon mashed avocado	Tropical Grains (page 147)	Pumpkin Spice Breakfast Rice (page 159)	Velvety Vanilla Brown Rice (page 141)	Buckwheat Cereal with Maple Apples (page 145)
Fruit/Veggie	Mashed pears	Blueberry Peary Sauce (page 128)	Slow Cooker Apples (page 48)	Mashed bananas		Raspberry Pear Sauce (page 135)	
Protein/ Other			Mashed scrambled eggs or egg yolks			1 teaspoon oatmeal	Yogurt
Lunch							
Cereal (Any cereal may be served as a lunch, but be sure to include a fruit/veggie, too.)							
Fruit/Veggie	Apples and Beets with Ginger (page 93)	Pears (page 55)	Peaches and Apples Sauce (page 132)	Green Beans (page 67)	Slow Cooker Apples (page 48) and diced avocado	Carrots for Everyone (page 63)	Sweet Potatoes (page 73)
Protein/ Other	Super Easy Chicken (page 80)	Polenta Cornmeal Mush Mash (page 160)	Brown rice with Diced Butternut Squash (page 189)	Three-Cheese Mac and Cheese (page 172)	Cut-up toast	Super Easy Chicken (page 80)	Fiesta Grains (page 174)

*Babies who are 8 to 10 months old are typically considered to be stage two, while babies who are 10 months of age and older are typically considered stage three.

**Your pediatrician may recommend that your baby eat commercial fortified infant cereal. If so, follow the recommendations on the box. A typical serving is 2 to 4 tablespoons.

Continued on next page.

Stages Two and Three Sample Meal Plan (continued)

Stage 2 and 3*	Sunday	Monday	Tuesday	Wednesday	Thursday	Friday	Saturday
Snacks: Offered up to twice per day	Peachy Pumpkin Sauce (page 133)	Mashed bananas and yogurt	Mixed fruit dices	Avocado dices with Slow Cooker Apples (page 48)	Dry cereal and diced fresh pears	Yogurt and peaches	Cut-up toast with Raspberry Pear Sauce (page 135) Peaches (page 54)
Dinner							
Cereal (Any cereal may be served as a lunch, but be sure to include a fruit/veggie, too.)							
Fruit/Veggie			Carrots and Black Beans (page 99)		Scalloped Sweet Potatoes with Apples (page 177)	Green Beans (page 67)	
Protein/ Other	Beef Stew (page 183)	Pork Tenderloin with Apples and Sweet Potatoes (page 166)	Super Easy Chicken (page 80)	Lentils and Beef with Carrots (page 167)	Haddock: Fish Ahoy! (page 81)	Fiesta Grains (page 174) and Lemon Chicken with Sweet Potatoes (page 165)	Creamy Dill Salmon with Peas (page 181)

*Babies who are 8 to 10 months old are typically considered to be stage two, while babies who are 10 months of age and older are typically considered stage three.

**Your pediatrician may recommend that your baby eat commercial fortified infant cereal. If so, follow the recommendations on the box. A typical serving is 2 to 4 tablespoons.

Continue to offer your baby her regular breast milk or formula feedings before giving her solid foods. (See "Suggested Daily Breast-Feeding or Formula-Feeding Schedule" below.)

Typical serving sizes for babies at stage two and three are
2–4 tablespoons of fruits
2–4 tablespoons of vegetables
2–4 tablespoons of protein such as chicken or beef
¼ to ½ cup of pasta, cereals, or other grains
¼ cup of yogurt
1 slice of toast or bread

Note that the schedule above is an example and doesn't need to be strictly followed. Also, the serving sizes above are guidelines; you should offer your baby as much as she will eat. Between the ages of 8 to 10 months old, babies begin to eat more solid foods, and many are eating three meals and having a snack each day as well. Be sure to consult your pediatrician about the proper menu and amounts for your baby.

Suggested Daily Breast-Feeding or Formula-Feeding Schedule

- 0–3 months of age: Breast-feed every 1–3 hours or feed 18–40 ounces of formula per day
- 4–5 months of age: Breast-feed every 2–4 hours or feed 24–45 ounces of formula per day
- 6–8 months of age: Breast-feed every 3–4 hours or feed 24–37 ounces of formula per day
- 9–12 months of age: Breast-feed every 4–5 hours or feed 24–31 ounces of formula per day

Resources

For additional information on a wide variety of topics pertaining to beginning your baby on solid foods, food safety, and more, consult these online resources.

Slow Cooker Food Safety:

https://www.extension.umn.edu/food/food-safety/preserving/safe-meals/slow-cooker-safety/

https://www.extension.umn.edu/food/food-safety/preserving/safe-meals/slow-cooker-safety/docs/factsheet.pdf

Safe Minimum Food Temperatures:

https://www.foodsafety.gov/keep/charts/mintemp.html

Information on Bisphenol A (BPA):

http://www.mayoclinic.org/healthy-lifestyle/nutrition-and-healthy-eating/expert-answers/bpa/faq-20058331

Salmon Facts:

http://seafood.edf.org/salmon

Phytochemicals and the Color of Foods:

https://www.fruitsandveggiesmorematters.org/what-are-phytochemicals

http://nutrition.ucdavis.edu/content/infosheets/factsheets/fact-pro-phytochemical.pdf

Starting Babies on Solid Foods—Infant Nutrition:

https://www.mayoclinic.org/healthy-lifestyle/infant-and-toddler-health/in-depth/healthy-baby/art-20046200

https://www.healthychildren.org/english/ages-stages/baby/feeding-nutrition/pages/switching-to-solid-foods.aspx

https://medlineplus.gov/infantandnewbornnutrition.html

Do's and Don'ts for Baby's Foods:

http://www.eatright.org/resource/food/nutrition/eating-as-a-family/dos-and-donts-for-babys-first-foods

USDA Nutrient Database:

https://ndb.nal.usda.gov/ndb/

Acknowledgements

Creating recipes and writing a cookbook is never easy. It takes a lot of ingredients, a lot of time, and a lot of testing. It also takes a whole clan of folks to bring a recipe book to publication. Dan Rosenberg at The Harvard Common Press reached out to me and asked if I'd be interested in creating a slow cooker baby food cookbook. I was skeptical, but he persisted and now . . . here we are! Thanks, Dan, for sharing your vision and for believing that I was the one bring it to life. And to Amy Kovalski; Amy was the best editor to have on a project like this. She was clear and concise and injected a bit of fun as well. It was lovely to work with you, Amy! Of course, without the patience and support of my family I never would have been able to sit down and actually write this book or have test-subjects. I love you all to pieces. Now, where did you hide the slow cooker?

About the Author

Maggie Meade is the creator of the website WholesomeBabyFood.com, which she started in 2003 and which is now part of the Momtastic network of sites. She has contributed to SheKnows.com, Babble.com, TheBump, CafeMom, *Oh Baby!* and *Baby Talk* magazine, among other outlets. She is the author of *The Wholesome Baby Food Guide*. She lives in New Hampshire with her husband and three children, and she continues to cook, write recipes, and maintain a digital brand.

Index

Capitalized entries are recipes.